T0341395

Praise for *Think Fast!*

"It's easy to get confused with all of the options facing most of us these days. With *Think Fast!*, Mr. Hale gives us an elegant, logical, and easy-to-use method for cutting through the clutter and making fast, reliable decisions."

—Dr. B. Lynn Ware
President & CEO, Integral Talent Systems, Inc.

"*Think Fast!* immediately transformed my ability to make good decisions with clarity and confidence. It makes sense. I just do what it says and get great results, every time. I refer back to it constantly in order to make this system a habit!"

—K. Walker
Founder and Publisher, Catholic Business Journal

"This remarkable book should have been written years ago. Guy Hale pleasantly and clearly shows us how to think better to achieve a much better result. This book is a must for anyone who wishes to become a more successful individual."

—Prammukti Surjaiudaja
CEO Bank NISP, Jakarta, Indonesia

"As an executive and management coach I often assign reading between coaching sessions. Now I have a resource for managers who want to improve their problem-solving or decision-making skills. Thank you!"

—Joe Tabers, CSP
Certified Speaking Professional and Executive Coach

Think
FAST!

ACCURATE
DECISION-MAKING,
PROBLEM-SOLVING,
and PLANNING
in MINUTES a DAY

Guy A. Hale

WILEY

John Wiley & Sons, Inc.

Published by John Wiley & Sons, Inc., Hoboken, New Jersey.
Published simultaneously in Canada.

Jacket and text designed by Ewa Krepsztul.

Bonus Chapter excerpt: "The Company Way" from *How to Succeed in Business Without Really Trying* by Frank Loesser © 1961 (Renewed) FRANK MUSIC CORP. All Rights Reserved. *Reprinted by Permission of Hal Leonard Corporation.*

For general information on our other products and services or for technical support, please contact our Customer Care Department within the United States at (800) 762-2974, outside the United States at (317) 572-3993 or fax (317) 572-4002.

Wiley also publishes its books in a variety of electronic formats. Some content that appears in print may not be available in electronic books. For more information about Wiley products, visit our website at www.wiley.com.

Library of Congress Cataloging-in-Publication Data

Hale, Guy A.

Think fast!: accurate decision-making, problem-solving, and planning in minutes a day / Guy Hale.

p. cm.

Includes index.

ISBN 978-1-118-00463-0 (hardback); ISBN 978-1-118-09651-2 (ebk); ISBN 978-1-118-09652-9 (ebk); ISBN 978-1-118-09653-6 (ebk)

1. Decision making. 2. Problem solving. 3. Critical thinking. 4. Management. I. Title.

HD30.23.H344 2011

658.4'03--dc22

2011011040

10 9 8 7 6 5 4 3 2 1

Contents

Foreword

Business leadership is more challenging now than ever before, due to hyper-competition, rapidly changing technology, and a raft of emerging players from every corner of the globe, who are pressuring companies to keep changing their game in order to survive and thrive. Evidence reveals that most companies are not responding well to these extra demands.

While there is no shortage of talent, past approaches to leadership come up short, leaving a serious shortage of effective leaders for today's environment. Author and organizational expert Guy Hale, in *Think Fast!*, begins to fill this vacuum by providing an easy-to-adopt, personal development system that addresses one of the most basic and crucial skills required for leading: effective thinking on the go.

Putting oneself on the line by making a decision requires courage and confidence because decisions imply taking responsibility, assuming accountability, and being open to criticism and failure. To gain the confidence (and overcome any fear) needed for effective decision making requires skill and practice. *Think Fast!* provides a new way to make consistent, well-thought-out decisions, in record time. And to make it easy for all, this new process comes complete with "how-to" templates and real life examples.

Although accurate thinking is the most frequently used of core leadership skills, Guy knows well that decision making alone is not sufficient. Confident, clear, problem-solving and planning skills are also critical, especially in today's fast-paced, highly competitive environment. And Guy delivers. He gives the reader excellent new tools and templates for fast, accurate problem solving and planning as well.

Guy's bonus chapter on Innovation, tucked way in the back of the book, is a useful extra once a reader has mastered the core leadership skills so excellently covered in this book. His promise of writing a new book on innovation will be in great demand.

The *Think Fast!* approach can easily be adopted by novices. It can be personalized and adapted to anyone's timetable. I would also recommend the book to more experienced leaders for skill improvement. Thanks to my years of first-hand CEO and VC experience, often being responsible for turning around corporate divisions and entire companies, I feel that I am a proven, capable, fast, and accurate decision maker, yet I was reminded, as I read this book, of steps I often overlook in order to be more consistent.

Guy has masterfully set a new standard for understanding, identifying, and developing key skills necessary for success. This book is a must have for those who have an interest in getting ahead in today's fast-paced and complex world.

Thomas Loarie
Executive Chairman
Mercator MedSystems, Inc.

Acknowledgments

My thanks to Lance Hale and Karen Walker for their tremendous contributions to this book. Without them this would not have been possible.

I'd also like to thank Shannon Vargo at John Wiley & Sons for her encouragement and coaching, and Ewa Krepsztul, who did a masterful job of designing the book.

Finally, I want to thank the many people from our client organizations who have given us so many good ideas.

One suggestion that we heard many times was that we should put the skills we teach into a short, easy-to-read book that everyone can relate to.

We listened carefully, and *Think Fast!* is the result.

Introduction

I know, you might be wondering how there could be a fast way of thinking. What good is fast if it isn't accurate? Besides, isn't thinking something we do (or don't do) every day without . . . uh . . . thinking about it?

Yes, and no.

Yes, you and I can't help using our gray cells every day. Even the poor soul who seems to make every wrong choice possible still uses some level of reasoning. The thinking might be distorted, or brilliant, or just plain wrong. But as humans, we can't help it. We all go through some type of reasoning process, whether deficient or robust, rash or plodding, to arrive at conclusions.

Okay, we need a process to ensure accurate decision making. But *accurate* without *fast*, in today's hyper-fast age of social networking and information overload, is not enough. None of us can spare time to ploddingly analyze situations and decisions. We need to think, accurately, on the fly. That's a tall order!

For some, fast and accurate execution of these skills seems impossible. But I assure you, this is not the case. You hold in your hand, at this very moment, a new way to look at something that may have seemed impossible just moments ago.

This book is your surest way to overcome the seemingly impossible with confidence, ease, and accuracy, every time.

That's a big promise.

I make it with confidence.

If you follow the system in this book, you will master decision making, problem solving, and planning with speed, ease, and accuracy, every time.

Your life will be richer for it!

Yes, the system found in these pages truly will give you a more stress-free, fulfilling, and rewarding life. To help you fulfill your dreams gives me great joy! This is why I'm delighted to share my new thinking with you. Think *Fast*!

Guy

Chapter One

GOOD NEWS

Knowing others is intelligence; knowing yourself is true wisdom. Mastering others is strength; mastering yourself is true power.

—Tao Te Ching

It is in self-imitation that a master first shows himself.

—Johann Wolfgang von Goethe,
German playwright, poet,
novelist, and dramatist, 1749–1832

A man who is master of himself can end a sorrow as easily as he can invent a pleasure.

I don't want to be at the mercy of my emotions.

I want to use them, to enjoy them, and to dominate them.

—Oscar Wilde,
Irish poet, novelist,
dramatist, and critic, 1854–1900

magine . . .

It's Monday morning. You're in the car, just heading to work after a two-week trip to Cancun.

On the way in, your cell phone hasn't stopped ringing, traffic is mostly stopped, and you can't imagine what must be waiting for you at the office. You feel your relaxed nerves slowly tightening.

Sure enough, just after greeting you with a hearty "Welcome back," the boss asks you to locate suitable office space "within the next two months" for a new foray into the Chicago region. You learn that Human Resources is behind schedule in downsizing (or "right-sizing," as the board likes to call it) 5 percent of the employees at two facilities, with a six-month deadline looming. And Sales and Marketing informs you that the personnel cuts are causing morale problems, which in turn threaten to adversely affect customer sales and perception.

And that's just the half of it. Thanks to right-sizing in other departments last year, you already feel like you have more on your plate than you can handle. What a day!

You arrive home exhausted. The relaxation you felt in Cancun is all but completely faded, and you go to bed early.

The next day, Tuesday morning, you take the train to work.

Well, at least you can respond to text messages on the train— that's a distinct advantage over driving! Small consolation. You're still wondering how to address your wife's new concerns about the big family move you decided to make to a new neighborhood. She wants to talk about it after dinner tonight. And then there's that urgent memo from the VP that came in just as you were leaving work yesterday. Now that you think of it, what are you going to do about your vacation resolution to "keep in shape no matter what"?

It hardly feels like you even had a vacation.

How often have you felt—at work or home—as though you had to act like everything is under control, but inside you are silently wondering how you're going to manage, how you're going to get it all done and on time?

You're not alone.

Like most of us, in this age of multitasking, information overload, and trying to juggle more responsibilities thanks to corporate downsizing—oops, I mean right-sizing—sometimes you just want to jump in the car and spend the day at the beach or by the lake, or hang out with friends, or go golfing, or go running, do *anything*, be *anywhere* else—just to get away from it all, clear your head, and try to gain some perspective.

Yes, after a mental break or physical activity, things do seem a little better. It's good to take a break. Yet the anxiety of trying to manage it all creeps quickly back and weighs even more heavily on your energy and spirit.

Wouldn't it be nice to have a simple system that made it all easy?

Even better, wouldn't it be nice to have a fast and easy system to juggle all these projects and demands?

"If only," you sigh, but you just arrived at work and must return to the projects at hand. Hey, is that your cell phone ringing again, or another text message?

Finally, you somehow manage to make it successfully through all the week's mountains. You feel tremendous relief—relaxation, even—and a sense of accomplishment. All the pressure that you felt at the beginning of the week is off your shoulders. You feel pounds lighter, lighter than air. It's almost as if those big Mount Everests of last week never existed. And after a little rest, you even feel a surge of newfound energy and an attitude of "I can do anything—bring it on!"

Then—BAM—slammed again. More deadlines, new goals, new mountains—the cycle repeats.

Is this what our leadership calls operating at optimum efficiency? Clearly this can't go on forever. I know a lot of my colleagues compare this new performance expectation to "feeling like they're on a hamster wheel," while trying to fit in eating, sleeping, and maintaining some kind of social life at the same time.

There must be a better way to deal with what's asked of you in life and work.

Believe me, I understand your pain!

When starting out in my career, I often felt the same way, overwhelmed beyond words. Soon I was juggling increasing corporate demands, a wonderful new, young and growing, family and a blur of projects, obligations, and dreams.

Like you, I wondered how I could keep it all together, keep making progress, and, frankly, stay sane in the process.

Don't get me wrong. I loved what I did. I still do. I love my family, too, which has always been the most important priority to me. Yet, even so, nothing changed how overwhelmed I often felt during those early years.

Then one day I made a breakthrough observation.

This observation led me to embark on a quest that resulted in the simple system you'll learn in this book: *a simple system that, once mastered, will enable you to achieve your goals and dreams with speed, ease, and confidence, and will greatly reduce your stress and worry.*

Imagine achieving what today seems overwhelming and impossible, with speed, ease, and confidence. Less stress and worry. It sounds like a dream come true.

THE OBSERVATION

One day it struck me that it must be possible to be successful in life and not feel constantly overwhelmed, because I had seen a handful of people who truly lived like this.

For me, these people were like seasoned mountain climbers, who are so skilled and confident in their ability to scale the tallest peaks that it almost seems to be second nature to them. They do things fast that would take me hours. I'm merely a weekend warrior who enjoys hiking. But merely observing the seasoned climber's level of expertise, confidence, and skill in mountain climbing—including how to handle outdoor emergencies and contingencies—was proof that if I ever desired to become an expert outdoor mountain climber, I knew at least it would be possible to gain this skill.

I learned something else from this observation. Both the seasoned mountain climber and the weekend hiker share something in common at the end of the journey. As they head down the mountain and back to the base camp, regardless of how steep or how rigorous the path, both veteran and weekender feel a sense of satisfaction, tired exhilaration, and relief, after accomplishing a great feat—almost as though the once-looming mountain is now easy.

The only difference between outdoor mountain climbing and the project mountains I faced every week at work, was that choosing to devote time and energy to climb the Himalayas or Mount Everest was a luxury for me. Whereas climbing my weekly mountain range of projects and responsibilities was not a luxury. It was a necessity.

People who exhibited these skills were like seasoned mountain climbers.

These few standout individuals always seemed to have it together, even though they juggled immense and highly demanding careers and responsibilities that were much greater than mine. Even in the midst of crises, these individuals exhibited a surprising sense of peace and calm clarity of thought and direction.

These individuals were not the ones clamoring for attention and stepping on others to promote themselves. Sometimes they weren't even the head of the department or company. And they didn't need a title to attract others to follow them.

Instead, these individuals were genuine leaders, anchors amid the chaos. They always seemed to have time to give an encouraging word, or to quickly redirect a project that had become derailed. Sometimes I'd come to these individuals to seek advice or to discuss a project. Always I'd walk away satisfied, at peace, because I had regained clarity about my concerns thanks to their comments.

That observation gave me hope. This was good news! After all, if these individuals could do it, so could I—but how?

Before we get to "how," it's important to ground ourselves in the good news that you and I—anyone who wants to—can master core thinking skills using a simple system that will eliminate the overwhelmed feelings that often plague us.

DO IT:

Go ahead, discover for yourself the same breakthrough that I had. This will give you practical evidence and hope that it is possible to have calm achievement in the face of great storms and responsibilities.

Write down the names of three people who seem to accomplish a lot with their lives, who are successful leaders, and yet who never seem to be overwhelmed in handling multiple responsibilities, or in facing new problems or challenges that come up. By leaders, I don't necessarily mean CEOs of multimillion-dollar companies. I mean people to whom others look for guidance and reassurance, steady anchors in a storm. These people may be from your work, your family, your church, or even someone you've observed at a favorite restaurant or somewhere else.

1. _____

2. _____

3. _____

Now take it a step further. Observe how these people address the onslaught of concerns that come their way. Write down your answers to these questions:

- How do these individuals maintain their composure in a crisis?

_____

_____

- How do these individuals get their group focused on the highest priority?

- How do these individuals initially respond to any concern presented?

- Were these individuals rational in their approach, or did they just react emotionally?

- How did these individuals make others feel when others offered their ideas?

Now, take a look at what you wrote.

If you want to become more like these people, the thinking skills you will learn from reading this book will help you get there.

YES, YOU CAN DO IT!

Over the years, I've seen countless people get off the hamster wheel and lead extraordinary lives of achievement—men and women of all ages, from senior executives and CEOs, to middle managers and new employees, to young parents, athletes, and entrepreneurs. And they did it because they embraced the simple system of thinking skills presented in this book. My hope is that you will have the same results. I know you can do it!

Take my word for it now, it *is* possible to achieve consistent clarity and calmness in the midst of whatever overwhelming and even unexpected projects and responsibilities come your way.

Let's look at how you, too, can master these same thinking skills with ease and confidence—and how you can do it in minutes a day.

TRUST THE PROCESS

Before we begin, I must insist on one thing: Trust the process!

If you trust the simple method I show you, you will discover—and truly master—problem solving, decision making, and planning so effectively that people will look to you as a leader. They will see you as a calm, steady, and effective guide, even through the toughest crisis situations. And, in truth, you will be just that. Others will want to emulate your qualities.

Now you might wonder, why should you trust me to guide you?

Let me tell you a quick story.

When I was first starting out on my career path, like most people, I wasn't exactly sure where I'd end up. Like you, each year it seemed that I faced increasing responsibilities—in life and at work—that required more thinking and management skills than I had.

Like you, I noticed that some senior executives and leaders exemplified how I wanted to be. They were calm, clear thinking, and effective, no matter what (or how much) came their way. They generated a reassuring sense of peace and direction and a can-do leadership approach that energized and focused others. Projects they managed ran smoothly, effectively, and on time. These projects were often even fun because we had real teamwork.

At the time, I knew inside that I did not possess these skills, but I wanted them. So I began a quest, with a small group of friends and colleagues who shared my observations.

Eventually we developed a foolproof system, based on observations, questions, time-consuming research, and relentless testing.

Now, having worked with tens of thousands of individuals, in literally thousands of companies nationwide and internationally, including individuals in more than 200 Fortune 500 companies, I can tell you that this system works.

On a personal level, I can tell you candidly that following this system has had one of the biggest impacts on my success in business and even in developing a harmonious family dynamic. It has made it possible to continue achieving my goals and dreams. And it has helped countless others as well, mainly corporate leaders and managers, whom my colleagues and I have had the privilege to train over the years, in the United States and around the world.

Again and again we witnessed furrowed brows on stressed-out employees, managers, and leaders at all levels, transform into grateful smiles. It never failed.

In writing this book, I simplify this system, these secrets of success, to make it even easier to possess the thinking skills of highly effective, productive leaders. By mastering these skills, you too will lead a satisfying, clear, and focused life—a life based on clear principles, not crazed reactions.

Are you ready?

Let's get started.

Chapter Two

START HERE: STOP

Thinking is the hardest work there is, which is the probable reason so few engage in it.

—Henry Ford

Even though the planet is round, there are just too many spots where you can find yourself hanging on to the edge just like I was; and unless there's some space, some place, to take a breather for awhile, the edge of the world—frightening as it is.

—Gloria Naylor,
African-American novelist and educator

You wouldn't fire a gun without aiming, would you?

So, why would we act without thinking . . .

Replacing thoughtful behavior with thoughtless acts leads to material, mental, and physical suffering: lost dreams, emotional turmoil, and bodily pain and illness.

—Chuck Gallozzi

To have a clear aim of where the action will lead is to be successful in everything . . .

Because of knowing the consequences of the actions before actually performing that action, he is able to continue putting in effort in spite of the challenges and difficulties.

So he continues to give his best to the task.

When he is able to give time to himself to think before performing any action, he is able to take the opportunity to be clear in his thinking. The consequences of the action he wishes to take are clear in his mind and so, the action taken to overcome the situation is right. Hence, he receives easy and sure success.

—Brahma Kumaris, Mt Abu

Things don't go wrong and break your heart so you can become bitter and give up. They happen to break you down and build you up so you can be all that you were intended to be.

—Samuel Johnson

"**H**uh?" you say. "You just got me ready to roll up my sleeves and get started learning how to master effective thinking skills, and now you tell me that the first step is to *stop*? I can't believe it!"

Yes, that's exactly what I'm saying. Start Here: Stop!

When faced with multiple projects or tasks, most people just jump right in with both feet. I suppose that's our natural tendency. We want to do something—*anything*—to change or alleviate a difficult or challenging situation. And when faced with many decisions or concerns at once, our natural tendency inclines us to try and put out fires as fast as we can, without taking a breath to think first.

There are some people who even deceive themselves into thinking that they did evaluate an issue or concern thoroughly prior to jumping in. But usually these people have not done so. There are many reasons for this—time constraints, deadlines, other demands, to name a few. Proof that they haven't sufficiently evaluated a situation before jumping in is in the result of their efforts.

The result is reactive. It is based on untested hunches, gut feelings, and unexamined intuition. Those aren't bad starting points, but they can never replace objective, systematic thinking.

What I call the knee-jerk reactionary approach is never productive. In fact, acting on our natural tendency to "just do something" puts us immediately onto the hamster wheel we spoke about in the first chapter. Not good.

If you don't seriously *stop* everything and take time out to look at, and assess, all the issues and concerns you face—big and small—that scream for your attention, you will never get off the hamster wheel. Never!

Let me give you an example.

CRITICAL RESPONSE TRAINING

What could be more demanding and overwhelming than the resulting demands after a physical catastrophe such as a major earthquake, a five-alarm fire, a terrorist attack, or a sinking cruise ship?

In the unfolding drama of such a major disaster, people react as they can—ducking for cover, running, grabbing life vests, whatever they can do to save and protect themselves and others.

Once that initial phase is over, our natural tendency to jump in and "put out fires" is strong.

Imagine the situation. You would hear screams for help, people in pain, people in horrific, desperate situations all around you. You see blood and people half-conscious, children crying for their parents. You want to help. You know you must do something, *anything*, to help those around you. You jump in and get to work, *without even thinking about it*.

But that's not what emergency Critical Response Training (CRT) experts and courses tell us to do. That's not the protocol for First Responders, those who arrive first on the scene of a catastrophic event. Just the opposite.

CRT experts teach us that the First Responders on any major disaster scene must quell their inner instinct to jump in and do what they can. Instead, they are trained to first assess the situation and group needs together. They are taught the first needs to look for, and how to prioritize among critical needs. And, given this protocol of first assessing the situation, these First Responders are able to achieve far more good than had they just jumped in with both feet.

Having first assessed the situation, according to a predetermined protocol, now these First Responders can group together those with the most severe among severe needs. They can direct others to help those in most need, assign groups to remove people from debris, send people for help or to get water, or to stop people's bleeding, and so forth.

It's simple logic, really. But it takes quelling our first natural, reactive instinct in order to allow logic to guide us.

The same is true in approaching an onslaught of overwhelming concerns, especially the kind that keep us up at night, and that have tight deadlines and weighty consequences.

Start Here: Stop.

DO IT:

Before we go further, let me get your commitment to stop the instant you begin to feel over your head.

I know it is tempting to skip this step. Yes, you understand, let's go on. But I assure you, if you do not take time to stop right now and fill in the following blanks, make a copy, and place it where you will always see it, then there's a real big chance that you likewise won't stop in the future . . . at a time when it's critical that you Start Here: Stop!

Fill in the following blanks:

> No matter how overwhelmed I feel, no matter how many deadlines and meetings I face, and no matter what the extenuating circumstances of the moment, I, _(your name)_, commit to always *begin by stopping* and immediately setting aside time to follow the process. I will not put this off. I will stop and take time out immediately.

Rewrite your commitment here:

Good job!

You're ready to learn what comes after Start Here: Stop!

REMEMBER:

- The *instant* you start to feel over your head with too much to do, *immediately* go to a quiet place in your office, home, or outside these locations. Turn off your phone ringer, close Facebook, Twitter, e-mail, and similar distractions. Close your door. Put a "Don't Interrupt" sign on it if you have to. Grab a pen and notebook, or your iPad, laptop, or smartphone, and . . .

STOP: START HERE.

Chapter Three

THE DUMP LIST

The discipline of writing something down is the first step toward making it happen.

—Lee Iacocca

By letting it go it all gets done. The world is won by those who let it go. But when you try and try. The world is beyond the winning.

—Lao Tzu

Courage is the power to let go of the familiar.

—Raymond Lindquist

've had people tell me this is their favorite step because it's so easy. They tell me it makes them feel great to get things out of their heads.

Once you've stopped immediately when faced with a challenge, new situations, or multiple concerns, the next thing to do is to create what I call a Dump List.

In this step, you must list all of your concerns on a piece of paper—or on a laptop or smartphone. And I mean *all* of your concerns. Just dump them out of your head.

Follow this format:

- List each concern on a separate line.
- Don't worry about complete sentences, grammatical structure, or details, just dump!

MEET JOHN

Consider the situation of one young executive, John. His is the story I had you imagine at the beginning of this book.

John had just returned to the office after a two-week vacation in Cancun. He showed up for work Monday morning refreshed and ready to go, only to be hit from all sides with urgent demands.

Poor John. To put it briefly:

> He returned to the office, in a way similar to the situation described in the first pages of this book, to learn that Human Resources were behind schedule in cutting another 5 percent of the employees at two facilities, with a six-month deadline looming. Sales and Marketing told him that the cuts were causing morale problems, and this in turn was affecting customer perception and sales. His boss put him in charge of opening a new office in Chicago within two months. His assistant wants to talk with him about taking off on pregnancy leave two months earlier than planned. Farmers were complaining about trees dying downstream from a Midwest plant.
>
> And there was more John had to deal with. A memo dated a week ago informed him that high-level French officials were arriving for a visit two weeks from today, and it was up to him to make sure the visit was a success. An e-mail and voicemail from the author of that memo wondered why he hadn't heard anything yet on a plan for the French. And, on top of it all, his spouse wanted to talk about their recent decision to move the family to a new home.
>
> Just as he hung up from his wife's call, he received another call, this one from the company's winery division. Their largest client, an airline, was ready to cancel all orders because the shape of the wine bottle was not space-efficient on the airlines. They were giving John's company four weeks to figure out a solution or good-bye.

One more project, in the back of his mind now, was that John had resolved during his two-week vacation to improve and stay in good physical shape. That was a new priority for him and he wanted to keep it. Where would he find the time, he wondered? Where would he find time to do his workouts, let alone take care of everything else?

John's situation might seem like an exaggeration, but it is not unusual. Whether you work for a big corporation or for yourself, the reality of getting slammed at work and in life is the same for all of us. More than that, it has become the new reality in this age of "right-sizing" and constant information overload, from the extra demands at work to the never-ending text messages and updates from Twitter, Facebook, and the like. It's just how it is.

Here's the key to making sense of it all.

It's not the responsibilities you are given, but rather, how you choose to handle these responsibilities that separates true leaders from the rest of the pack.

Lucky for John, he has some mastery of our easy thinking system.

Let's see how he does.

JOHN'S SITUATION

At first John was beside himself with anxiety. How could he possibly address all these things at once? All he wanted to do was take the quickest plane back to his island vacation. Who could blame him?

Then he remembered: Start Here: Stop. And he did so. Right there and then.

John stopped his fretting. He asked his assistant to hold all calls. He closed his e-mail and turned off his cell phone. And, most important of all, John quelled his desire to jump right in. Instead, he set aside 45 minutes of uninterrupted time.

When John relayed his story to me much later, I asked him what he would do if he didn't have an office door to shut or an assistant to hold calls.

"I'd go out for an hour somewhere—a coffee shop, the local library, a park," he told me without hesitating. "I would go anywhere quiet where I could stop and take time to assess things in a focused way."

Now what?

MAKING THE DUMP LIST

Now John did the next step. He had already stopped and taken time. Now he wrote his Dump List. He just emptied out onto a piece of paper all of the concerns and demands swirling around in his mind, all the things he had to deal with, all the "urgencies" and "not so urgencies" that cried out for his attention.

These days John often uses his iPad or laptop instead of a sheet of paper, but it doesn't matter. The point is that he literally dumped out all that was on his mind.

John remembered to list each concern on a separate line.

His Dump List looked something like this:

- Reduce head count in target facilities
- Poor morale in sales and marketing
- Find out cause of dying trees near Midwest plant
- New office space in Chicago within two months
- French visit
- New home for family
- Jessica's pregnancy leave
- Replacement for Jessica—2 months
- Stay physically fit
- Wine bottles and storage

DO IT:

Write your own Dump List. Remember, one line for every concern or situation you currently face. Just dump it on paper, or use the following blanks.

_____

_____

_____

_____

_____

_____

_____

Did you miss anything? No? Good!

It's been pretty easy so far, hasn't it?

Now you're ready for the next step in our system.

REMEMBER:

- As soon as you are in your quiet zone, just pour out all of your concerns. Write them down in your notebook, iPad, or similar device. Don't think about it, just get them out of your head and onto paper or computer.

- List each concern on a separate line.

CREATE YOUR DUMP LIST

Chapter Four

SIMPLIFY

Everything should be made as simple as possible, but not simpler.

—Albert Einstein

Beware the barrenness of a busy life.

—Socrates

The ability to simplify means to eliminate the unnecessary so that the necessary may speak.

—Hans Hofmann,
Introduction to the Bootstrap, 1993

The sculptor produces the beautiful statue by chipping away such parts of the marble block as are not needed—it is a process of elimination.

—Elbert Hubbard

Any intelligent fool can make things bigger, more complex, and more violent. It takes a touch of genius—and a lot of courage—to move in the opposite direction.

—E. F. Schumacher

I am convinced that to make something simple is at once the most difficult and easiest skill of all. It is difficult for one who doesn't have a system to filter through the noise and get quickly to the heart of the matter. Yet it is easy for a person who does have such a system.

Let me give you a quick example.

How many times have you been in a meeting where ideas and proposed solutions to a problem began flying around the room like a windstorm, fast and furious? Then, amid the intense discussion and counterproposals and "what ifs," a calm, confident voice interjects a summary that is spot-on. It literally takes everyone's breath away. It is so clear.

Maybe that interjecting voice starts with something like this: "So, let's take a look at where we are. We have five proposals on the table: Number One, Number Two, Number Three . . . "

The room is quickly silent. A few people say, "Exactly!" "That's right!" "uh-huh, yeah . . . "

Then the calm voice continues, "Great. Now if we look at each of these more closely, we can see that Number Two and Number Five are similar except for this one thing (which he explains), so we can call this entire proposed idea Number Two, with alternatives A and B. Would you agree?"

"Yes, sure." "Right."

The calm confidence continues, as this person quickly guides the group to examine, evaluate, and organize each of the proposals. This input is critical to moving forward and actually resolving the issue. This person clarified and simplified all the proposals on the table. Without this simplifying process, that windstorm of ideas would never result in clarity or meaningful action.

So, how can you get good at simplifying things, especially if that's not your best talent? No worries. This skill is easily acquired with practice. The first two steps—Start Here: Stop and the Dump List—have already put you on the path to simplifying.

Consider John again. He did a good job of writing down all the concerns that had been swirling around in his head. Now he's ready to simplify. He merely goes back over his list to make sure that he has one item on each line.

Simplify: One item and one action verb for each concern.

To put it another way, one single action on your part must be all that is needed to check off and resolve each item listed. Some of your concerns may require more action to ultimately be resolved, but they don't require more action from you. Remember, you are writing *your* Dump List, not someone else's.

A quick and easy way to simplify any Dump List is to ask this question for each item: *Will one action resolve this concern?*

Sometimes you'll find that an item needs to be broken up into smaller, preliminary items. After all, as the old saying goes, you can't eat an elephant in one bite.

How did John simplify his list?

John's list is a great example. Let's go through it quickly so you'll see how he simplified it.

- Reduce head count in target facilities.

  Simplify: Will one action resolve this concern?

  Answer to the question: Probably not. John knows that Human Resources has already fallen behind its schedule, so he suspects that there's a reason for this. But he doesn't know why the department fell behind. It might be that circumstances or personnel have changed in the department since the original plan was made. It might be that the facilities are struggling with where and how to cut. Or, it could be something else. At any rate, one action won't solve this concern. So John changes it—simplifies it—to read:

  - Talk with HR to learn why reduction plan is behind schedule.
  - Meet with HR to adjust plan in order to meet six-month deadline.
  - Set up benchmark dates with HR to reevaluate progress.

Good job! Now John can easily act on those simplified items to resolve his Dump List concern. What's next on his list?

- Poor morale in sales and marketing.

Simplify: Will one action resolve this concern?

Answer to the question: No. This concern is too vague. It's like an elephant that can't be eaten in a single bite. Or, a better analogy, it's like a mountain peak that can't be hiked in a single day.

What does the sales and marketing department mean when they tell John that there is poor morale? John needs to understand—in a concrete way—what is meant by poor morale.

It would be easy to assume that poor morale means that employees at the two targeted facilities are worried about their own job security and are spending work time looking for other work. But it could also mean that with the reduction in manufacturing, sales and marketing employees are losing confidence in the company's ongoing ability to fulfill its product delivery obligations. Or, it could mean that sales and marketing think the company is unfair in some way. At any rate, John doesn't know the answer to this question, so he breaks his concern down further—*he simplifies it*—to read:

- Find out why sales and marketing employees have poor morale.

Much better! Now John can resolve this concern with a single action. Let's continue through John's Dump List.

- Find out cause of dying trees on farms near Midwest plant.

Simplify: Will one action resolve this concern?

Answer to the question: Yes. Once John finds out why, then this concern is resolved.

Next on John's list:

- New office space in Chicago within two months.

Simplify: Will one action resolve this concern?

Answer to the question: Maybe. First, John notices that he doesn't have an action verb, so he adds one. His new item becomes:

- *Find* new office space in Chicago within two months.

Okay, that's better. John knows that if he assigns a person to this job, *his* concern can be resolved by a single action. John therefore simplifies his concern again to read:

- Assign person to find new office space in Chicago within two months.

Good. Now this item can be resolved with one action on his part. John continues down his list.

- French visit.

Simplify: Will one action resolve this concern?

Answer to the question: Maybe. "French visit" is too vague. Yes, John knows what he means, vaguely. But if he really wants to simplify his list, he must add an action verb and clarify his concern. He fixes his concern to read:

- *Plan* French officials' visit *by Friday.*

Fantastic! John is already feeling the weight come off his shoulders. And you are probably beginning to see the pattern of simplifying John's list too. At least the system of simplifying is getting easier for you. Let's keep going.

> • New home for family.

> *Simplify:* Will one action resolve this concern?
>
> *Answer to the question:* Do you already know the answer to this question? John recognizes that one action will not yet resolve this concern. He also sees that there is no action verb. John also knows that this concern involves a discussion with his wife, so he quickly rephrases his item to read:
>
> → • Set aside time this week with Alicia to discuss new home for family.

Now this item can be resolved with one action.

Next on John's Dump List:

> • Jessica's pregnancy leave.

> *Simplify:* Will one action resolve this concern?
>
> *Answer to the question:* Clearly not.

DO IT:

How would you simplify this concern for John?

Here's how John simplified this concern:

  • Set aside time to talk with Jessica today or tomorrow about her pregnancy leave dates.

You may have noticed that resolving this item needs to be broken down. But if you looked over John's list, you also noticed that his next item is related to this concern. In other words, when John was creating his quick Dump List, he happened to break down this concern already. Good job!

Next on John's list:

  • Replacement for Jessica—2 months.

  Simplify: Will one action resolve this concern?

  Answer to the question: Not yet. John quickly fixed his list item to read:

  • Launch replacement search process with Human Resources (HR).

He continues. John's next item reads:

  • Stay physically fit.

  Simplify: Will one action resolve this concern?

  Answer to the question:

DO IT:

How would you answer this question for John?

DO IT:

How would you simplify John's concern?

John simplified his item this way:

> • Make physical fitness plan.

Now it's easy to take care of this item in one action. It's getting easier to simplify items, isn't it?

Last on John's list:

• Wine bottles and storage.

Simplify: "Will one action resolve this concern?

Answer to the question: As you can easily recognize now, John's item is too vague. It cannot be resolved with one action. John knows that he will delegate this item to Research and Development (R&D), but he also knows that he must be very clear in describing the problem that the airline is having with the wine bottles. He also knows that he must keep on top of this item throughout the process since the company can't afford to lose one of its biggest clients, and the timeline for resolution is very tight. So John clarifies and simplifies his Dump List concern like this:

> • Find out details on airline space limitations.

Done. That didn't take long!

John looks again at his simplified Dump List. He's made a lot of progress in a short amount of time. And, just like the First Responders in a crisis situation, John has taken the time to apply a proven process to the many concerns he needs to address. Now he feels ready to tackle them one at a time.

Here's what John's Simplified Dump List looks like now. Note that the Dump List is slightly longer, but John's concerns are now defined in a way that he can easily address them:

- Talk with HR to learn why reduction plan is behind schedule.
- Meet with HR to adjust plan in order to meet six-month deadline.
- Set up benchmark dates with HR to reevaluate progress.
- Find out why sales and marketing employees have poor morale.
- Find out cause of dying trees on farms near Midwest plant.
- Assign person to find new office space in Chicago within two months.
- Plan French officials' visit by Friday.
- Set aside time this week with Alicia to discuss new home for family.
- Set aside time to talk with Jessica today or tomorrow about her pregnancy leave dates.
- Launch replacement search process with Human Resources (HR).
- Find out details on airline space limitations.
- Make physical fitness plan.

DO IT:

Now that you've had some practice, take a look at your own Dump List and simplify it. I know you'll find that you can do it with ease. Remember, for each item on your list, ask: "Can this be resolved by one action?" If the answer is "no," then clarify or break down the item until it (or its subitems) can be resolved with one action. Make sure you have included one action verb for each concern listed.

MY DUMP LIST—SIMPLIFIED

MAKE IT EVEN SIMPLER: PRIORITIZE

Great job so far! Now, you must go back quickly over your Simplified Dump List and assign a priority to each item.

What kind of prioritizing system do you use?

Yes, I know that there are several types of priority systems. But let's keep it simple. I'm just going to recommend what we've seen work the best: the simple 1–10 scale. "1" means a concern is the lowest priority, and "10" indicates it's the highest.

Of course, any item that must be resolved within one or two days is a much higher priority than something that must be achieved a few months from now. But, be careful.

Be attentive. Some items, such as John's need to resolve the wine bottles storage issue for one of his largest clients, have a deadline of four weeks. But if he doesn't start immediately on this item, he won't allow enough time for R&D to come up with new solutions to present to the client. That makes starting the process to address this issue one of the highest priorities, in spite of its ultimate four-week deadline.

DO IT:

Take a stab at prioritizing John's Simplified Dump List, using whatever prioritizing system works for you.

Here is a tip to make assigning 1–10 priorities easier: Find the most critical concern on your list and give it a "10." Remember, this is your only list, so choose one item and assign it a "10."

Once you've assigned your "10" item, the other items should fall more easily into place. All you have to do now is quickly compare each remaining concern to your "10." On the 1–10 scale, how does each item compare in priority to your "10"?

This becomes very quick and easy after a few tries.

PRIORITY (1–10; 10 is highest)	JOHN'S SIMPLIFIED DUMP LIST
	Talk with HR to learn why reduction plan is behind schedule.
	Meet with HR to adjust plan in order to meet six-month deadline.
	Set up benchmark dates with HR to reevaluate progress.
	Find out why sales and marketing employees have poor morale.
	Find out cause of dying trees on farms near Midwest plant.

Assign person to find new office space in Chicago by Thanksgiving.

Plan French officials' visit by Friday.

Set aside time this week with Alicia to discuss new home for family.

Set aside time to talk with Jessica today or tomorrow about her pregnancy leave dates.

Launch replacement search process with Human Resources.

Find out details on airline space limitations.

Make physical fitness plan.

Here's how John prioritized his list:

PRIORITY	JOHN'S SIMPLIFIED DUMP LIST
⑦	Talk with HR to learn why reduction plan is behind schedule.
⑥	Meet with HR to adjust plan accordingly in order to meet six-month deadline.
⑥	Set up benchmark dates with HR to reevaluate progress.
⑧	Find out why sales and marketing employees have poor morale.
⑧	Find out cause of dying trees on farms near Midwest plant.

⑨	Assign person to find new office space in Chicago within two months.
⑩	Plan French officials' visit by Friday.
⑨	Set aside time this week with Alicia to discuss new home for family.
⑧	Set aside time to talk with Jessica today or tomorrow about her pregnancy leave dates.
⑦	Launch replacement search process with Human Resources.
⑧	Find out details on airline space limitations.
⑤	Make physical fitness plan.

DO IT:

Now, assign a priority to each item on your list.

PRIORITY	MY DUMP LIST—SIMPLIFIED

Remember when you first started this book? You might have felt overwhelmed. But now you have quickly advanced to having a simple list of actionable items, with a priority assigned to each item.

Your concerns are no longer vague or confusing or overwhelming. Instead, they are concrete, practical, actionable, and you know in which order to address them. Already life is simpler, easier, and the view ahead, much clearer!

REMEMBER:

- Look at your Dump List, one concern at a time.
- Ask: Will one action resolve this concern?
    - If the answer is yes, then move on to the next concern.
    - If the answer is no, then simplify it. Break it down into several concerns, if needed. Make sure that each concern has only one action verb and one object.
- Assign a 1–10 priority to each concern.
    - 1 is least urgent; 10 is most urgent.
    - Identify the 10 first. Rate everything in relation to the urgency of that 10.

SIMPLIFY AND PRIORITIZE

Chapter Five

PICK THE RIGHT ROAD: THREE LITTLE QUESTIONS

If you do not ask the right questions, you do not get the right answers.

A question asked in the right way often points to its own answer.

Asking questions is the A-B-C of diagnosis. Only the inquiring mind solves problems.

—Edward Hodnett, poet (1841–1920)

Effective management always means asking the right question.

—Robert Heller

N ow that you've taken time to write out and simplify your Dump List . . . . Now that all the concerns that were swimming madly around in your head not too long ago are on paper (or in your smartphone or computer), simplified, and prioritized, now you must pick the right road for each concern and get to work . . .

To give you a little encouragement here, you've already done the most challenging part (that was Step One: Stop).

Okay, you'll now look at each simplified concern and pick the right road for it.

What does "right road" mean?

Let me explain. Just as a driver must define the right road to take in order to arrive at his desired destination, so you must pick the right road for each of your concerns in order to resolve them. If you pick the wrong road, you won't resolve your concern.

Do not skip this step! Making sure that each concern is on the right road is a critical step if you want to truly master accurate decision making, problem solving, and planning.

I can't tell you how many people I've observed who jump right in trying to resolve their concerns, yet without first making sure they are on the right road. These people waste hours of time, sometimes days, fumbling around.

But not you!

Instead, in this book I'm giving you the secrets of *mastering* the three key thinking skills. And one of the biggest secrets is also one of the most subtle: You must pick the right road for each concern.

This step greatly speeds up your progress. It ensures you are on the correct path to resolving each of your concerns. No fumbling around and wasting time.

PICK THE RIGHT ROAD

Picking the right road for each concern is easy. You just identify which thinking skill you'll need to use in order to resolve each concern. That's it.

Don't worry, I'll teach you how to apply the three main thinking skills later. For this step, you only need to pick the right road to resolve each concern. Nothing else.

You need to know—at a glance—when you look at each concern—whether you need to:

- Decide something
- Find out why
- Make a plan

This is easy. It will take you five minutes (at most) to read through your list and pick the right road for each concern, using the three questions I'll teach you.

I'm sure the results of this quick categorizing process are clear to you. Once you know which skill is needed to resolve each concern, then you can tackle your Dump List with no worries or stress, but instead with ease and confidence.

Because picking the right road is such an important step in the secret of confident, stress-free achievement, I want to explain a little more fully.

There are basically three thinking skills we use to solve most of our concerns in life:

1. Decision making: Decide now

2. Problem solving: Find out why

3. Planning: Plan to make it happen

These three thinking skills are like the plays in football or basketball.

For example, if you ever played or now follow the great sport of football, you know that a team practices several key plays to address several different challenges from an opponent. When the team is in the heat of the game, they can apply these plays when needed.

Let's say the quarterback (QB) approaches the line of scrimmage and he sees that the opponent has a different defensive set than what his team expected. The QB calls an audible (shouts a code) to let his teammates know that they're going to run a different play than what they'd planned in the huddle, in order to exploit the opponent's change in defense.

If the QB is at the line of scrimmage and he sees that the opponent is going to blitz, he quickly shouts an audible to indicate he's changing his team's play to something else, say a screen pass, in order to exploit the blitz and get the long gain or a touchdown.

Maybe football isn't your game. That's okay. The analogy still applies.

If you're a basketball fan, just like in football or any sport, you know that your team has repeatedly practiced several different plays in order to address different strategies that the opposing team might use against you.

For example, when you see that the opponent is going to press your team (trying to attack every team member so that your team will lose the ball to the possession of your opponent), then your team will respond to the press with screens; doubling up against the opponent who is blocking your teammate who has the ball so that, in a split second, your player can break free and hopefully run down the court for a shot. Your team needs different plays, based on the different situations your opponent might throw at you.

But perhaps the best analogy of all is in golf. If you're a golf fan, you know that you must decide which club to use based on where you are on the course, the position of the ball in relation to your feet, and the type of surface you're on—fairway, sand trap, or in the rough.

You need to use a different club for each different kind of situation you might face. In the same way, you need to use a different thinking skill for each different kind of concern you face. Using the same thinking skill all the time just doesn't work.

Put simply, asking the three little questions for each concern is like deciding which club you need to use in order to resolve each concern on your Dump List.

"Oh, that's simple," you say.

And you're right!

But be sure that you don't skip this step just because it is simple. When you pick the right road for each concern, using the following three little questions I teach you, you move much more quickly and confidently toward resolving each item on your list.

Let's begin.

Look at each item on your list, one by one, and ask yourself these three little questions:

- Do I need to make a decision? (Decide now?)
- Do I need to find the cause? (Why?)
- Do I need to plan to make it happen? (How?)

John quickly reviews his simplified list and writes down which of the three little questions applies to each concern.

John's list now looks like this:

⑦	Talk with HR to learn why reduction plan is behind schedule.	Find cause: WHY?
⑥	Meet with HR to adjust plan in order to meet six-month deadline.	Plan to Make it Happen: HOW?
⑥	Set up benchmark dates with HR to reevaluate progress.	Plan to Make it Happen: HOW?
⑧	Find out why sales and marketing employees have poor morale.	Find cause: WHY?
⑧	Find out cause of dying trees on farms near Midwest plant.	Find cause: WHY?
⑨	Assign person to find new office space in Chicago within two months.	Make decision: DECIDE NOW
⑩	Plan French executives' visit by Friday.	Plan to Make it Happen: HOW?
⑧	Set aside time this week with Alicia to discuss new home for family.	Make Decision: DECIDE NOW
⑦	Set aside time to talk with Jessica today or tomorrow about her pregnancy leave dates.	Make Decision: DECIDE NOW
⑦	Launch replacement search process with Human Resources.	Plan to Make it Happen: HOW?
⑧	Find out details on airline space limitations.	Find cause: WHY?
⑤	Make physical fitness plan.	Plan to Make it Happen: HOW?

DO IT:

Now, pick the right road for each item on your list, using the three little questions.

PRIORITY	MY DUMP LIST	THREE LITTLE QUESTIONS

REMEMBER:

- Identify the thinking skill needed to resolve each concern by asking three simple questions for each concern:

  - Do I need to make a decision? (Decide now?)

  - Do I need to find the cause? (Why?)

  - Do I need to plan to make it happen? (How?)

    PICK THE RIGHT ROAD: THREE LITTLE QUESTIONS

Chapter Six

RECOGNIZE
YOUR PROGRESS

Celebrate any progress. Don't wait to get perfect.

—Ann McGee Cooper

Take pride in how far you have come, have faith in how far you can go.

—Author Unknown

Great job!

Take a quick second to savor how much progress you've made.

You, or at least John, started out feeling overwhelmed, with concerns crowding out the ability to think and act clearly. It felt like swimming against the tide without a break. Each day seemed to bring new concerns, yet the old ones weren't resolved yet. Work was tough enough, but there were important family relationships that needed attention, too. How were you supposed to handle it all, and more? When could you take time to stay healthy and fit, grow in your passions and hobbies, help and lead at your church or synagogue, pursue your dreams? How could you ever get ahead?

Now, within only an hour or so—maybe only 30 minutes—your life has radically changed for the better.

Look at your list.

You've tamed all of your concerns.

Each one is listed, simplified, prioritized, and on the right road to be resolved.

You're breathing easier. Stress has slipped away.

You're confident now that if you get slammed with more responsibilities, you can handle them. You have a system. You will immediately Start Here: Stop! and follow the process through to this point.

You've made a lot of progress!!

Yet it was easy!

I'm proud of you. Even more, you should be proud of yourself! Soon colleagues and others will be wondering what your secret is for calm leadership. You can count on it. And remember, I'm here with you every step of the way to keep you on track.

Now what?

GOING FORWARD

Now you're ready to act. You're ready to tackle your list and handle each concern. And that means you're ready to learn how to execute each thinking skill in the most effective way possible.

In the next three chapters, I teach you the secrets to executing the following three thinking skills effectively and with confidence:

1. Make a decision: Decide now!

2. Find out the cause: Why?

3. Plan to make it happen: How?

Trust me. You're making terrific progress toward developing the systems and habits that will enable you to handle every concern—big or small—that comes your way, and to achieve your dreams!

Let's begin.

Chapter Seven

PRESENT: DECIDE NOW!

It does not take much strength to do things, but it requires great strength to decide on what to do.

—Elbert Hubbard

The roads we take are more important than the goals we announce.

Decisions determine destiny.

—Frederick Speakman

The indispensable first step to getting the things you want out of life is this: Decide what you want.

—Ben Stein

Once you make a decision, the universe conspires to make it happen.

—Ralph Waldo Emerson

When you come to a fork in the road, take it.

—Yogi Berra

No trumpets sound when the important decisions of our life are made. Destiny is made known silently.

—Agnes de Mille

Leadership begins with self-knowledge.
Life decisions can be good decisions only if they hit your own personal bedrock.

—Vince Lombardi

Making a decision is the most commonly used thinking skill we humans execute daily. You make decisions every day, from whether to brush your teeth in the morning, which clothes to wear to work, and what to have for breakfast, to what time you'll leave the office, whether you'll fly out to visit a friend or attend a seminar, and how much money you'll set aside each month for an emergency fund or for investing.

Some of the decisions you make are so habitual you don't even think about them, such as brushing your teeth or saying "thank you" when given a gift or when someone does something nice for you.

Other decisions take more time and thought, such as buying a car or considering a new job or opportunity.

And a few decisions seem agonizing to make, such as whether to attend a friend's out-of-town wedding, or which person to trust in a sensitive matter, or what to do about a difficult personnel or family situation.

But don't worry. Making a good decision is easy once you learn a few secrets. The first secret is that making any decision—whether simple or agonizing—requires the same simple process.

Let me explain.

Every decision involves a choice between one or limitless items.

For example, we could choose to brush our teeth or chew gum.

We could choose to attend a friend's wedding or just send a gift.

In traveling to another state, we could choose this flight, or that one, or another time, or another airline, or take a train, or drive, or . . . (nearly limitless).

An easy decision-making system gives us quick focus to make good, accurate decisions with consistency, every time.

I must emphasize this point. The system you'll learn here will teach you how to make good, accurate decisions every time. Not just any decision, but good decisions. Not just now and then, but every time.

You and I make decisions every day. Yet, how accurate are they? How strong are these decisions? Do they hold up to the test of time and results?

Let me give you an example. A friend of mine seems to have a knack for buying bad cars. Every time, he does the same thing. He gets to the point where he decides it's time to trade in his current car for a new one. The repair expenses warrant it. Then he and his wife go car hunting. They don't write anything down ahead of time. They don't take a realistic look at their budget. They don't get different estimates on the value of their current car. They don't save for a down payment. They don't spend a dime to look up the repair history of the car using its unique VIN number. "What a waste of time and money," they say. They don't really think much about it.

Instead, this couple goes car hunting with a sense of urgency and a vague notion that they need a vehicle to hold their family of five and maybe some of their dogs now and then, and they want any monthly payments to be low. They figure their down payment will be the trade-in value of the car they now own; that is, the trade-in value the dealer offers them. Pretty vague!

I've seen these dear people buy new cars and used cars, always with the same result: They aren't satisfied after a few months. Either the new car has bigger monthly payments than they comfortably can afford (even though it seemed reasonable in the dealer's office), or the car can't accommodate their family and their dogs, or even one extra person, at the same time; or the car starts showing signs of needing repair within the first three months of ownership.

It saddens me to see my friend go through this process time and time again. But there it is.

The good news is that you don't have to follow my friend's sad example.

CONSISTENTLY GOOD, ACCURATE DECISIONS

When my colleagues and I were studying this process, we observed that in order to consistently make a good, accurate decision, there are a few things a person must do every time he or she makes a decision.

Good decision making requires:

- Knowing the purpose for the decision.

- Knowing which factors are negotiable and which are nonnegotiable.

- Knowing how each different option compares only to your criteria.

- Identifying and assessing risks involved with each option.

That's it.

But beware. If just one of these requirements is missing, the resulting decision is not clear and usually not well grounded. That means it can come back to bite you, like the car-buying habits of my friend. You don't want that. Instead, you want to make good decisions with confidence.

Here's an easy way to remember the four components of decision making:

1. Purpose: What's the purpose of the decision?

2. Criteria: What are the negotiable and nonnegotiable factors?

3. Compare to criteria: How does each option (alternative choice) measure up?

4. Risks: What are the risks associated with each option? How serious are they?

DON'T SKIP A STEP . . . NOT A SINGLE STEP!

Believe me, I know how tempting it is to skip a step here. You might have a vague notion of the purpose or criteria for a decision—"It's obvious, isn't it?" You might just instinctively gravitate to one or another of the options before you. And, worst of all, you might just jump right in with both feet and start paddling. Not good.

"But I know what I want to do," you say. "It's clearly option C."

Okay, fine. But if it's a work-related decision, your manager, client, or CEO might ask you to justify your decision. Maybe he or she won't ask you to justify your decision until several months later, after a project bombed. To respond, "It just felt right" or "It was clear at the time" won't cut it. (Keep in mind my sad car-buying friend.)

If you're like another friend of mine, you might be highly intuitive. It's remarkable; this friend gets it right 8 times out of 10! But even so, this friend is not a calm, effective leader. The evidence is most apparent when it comes to bigger projects. Her purpose is sometimes obscured. Nonnegotiables are vague. Things with this person in charge are hectic and seat-of-the-pants. Risks aren't identified ahead of time with any clarity, so any challenges that come up are unanticipated. And if ever asked to justify a decision, the response isn't pretty.

Remember the sports analogies from an earlier chapter? The same applies here.

Imagine a football or basketball coach who doesn't anticipate possible opponent moves ahead of game time. Imagine a QB who shouts out an audible because "it seems likely," without quickly and accurately assessing the opponent's strategy. Imagine the golfer who "just wings it" when he pulls out a club for a putt or a drive. The results would be absurd, like a cartoon in the funny papers. I know I sure wouldn't want a stockbroker or doctor who makes decisions this way!

YES BUT . . .

If you're someone who understands the point, but who nonetheless is overwhelmed at the thought of going through four steps to make a decision, take heart.

Use these four steps every time you need to make a decision, and you'll soon notice a remarkable result: It becomes a habit! Just like brushing your teeth.

These four steps will quickly define how you make decisions. so that in a few weeks you wouldn't think of not including every step.

A LESSON FROM THE PROS

When I played baseball in college, one of our star pitchers signed on with a major league club. As you can imagine, that was exciting for all of us .

Later, I learned something from this pitcher that really surprised me. He told me that he—like every professional baseball pitcher during their first season in pro baseball—had to relearn his pitching skills. Like all other players chosen to play for a professional team for the first time, my teammate was assigned to the pro team's minor league club in order to hone his natural ability before advancing to the major league team.

Bottom line: Our star pitcher had to relearn his pitching skills in order to make it to the major league. I was shocked! Wasn't it his very skill at pitching that earned him a place on the pro team?

It didn't make sense. Why would a star baseball pitcher who earned his way to pro baseball have to relearn his pitching skills?

The reason is simple: To ensure that this pitcher will be consistently good at pitching—to ensure he will be a pitcher and not merely a thrower—he had to understand every component, every nuance, and every secret, of pitching.

My teammate had to learn how to pitch to each different kind of hitter. He had to be precise in his skills. If he needed to pitch a strike, for example, he needed to be able to do that on demand. He had to understand exactly what he needed to do in order to place the ball in the strike zone, and he had to have a change-up.

Having a 90-mile-per-hour fastball and a curve is not enough once you're playing in the big leagues. My college teammate needed to relearn how to pitch in order to be consistent, even on days when he didn't have his best stuff.

Playing baseball in the major leagues is much more grueling and demanding than at any other playing level, no matter how much practice, sacrifice, and skill a player may have. At the major league level, there's too much riding on every game, every win, every play, every season, so there's no room for inconsistency. How much a team owner can (or can't) afford to put into next season's draft picks, and many other things, depend on how the team performs in every game.

In the major leagues, a pitcher must consciously think about and understand every component of pitching. Instinct alone won't allow him to be a star at the major league level. When he makes a bad throw in a game, he must be able to self-correct on the spot.

The same is true for all of us—in the board room, on the field, and in family and day-to-day life. Instinct and vague intuition won't carry the day, with consistent accuracy, every time.

Remember this: Good instincts alone will never yield the same consistent good results we want to have. A person with good instincts will be an even better—a more reliable—decision maker with the use of the system presented in this chapter.

JOHN'S DECISION MAKING

Let's go back to John's list. He only had three concerns that will require the decision-making skill:

1. Assign person now to find new office space in Chicago within two months.

2. Set aside time this week with Alicia (John's wife) to discuss new home for family.

3. Set aside time to talk with Jessica today or tomorrow about her pregnancy leave dates.

Each of these decision-making concerns is fairly straight-forward.

John assigns Angela, his assistant customer service manager, to find new office space in Chicago. He decides he'll call his wife at noon today to set up a time when they can discuss the new family home. He lets his assistant, Jessica, know that they can talk about her pregnancy leave tomorrow at 10 am. Done.

Thanks to the simplification of his Dump List, these three concerns are now scheduled to be resolved.

To see how the decision-making system works, let's go back and consider John's first decision-making concern—finding new office space in Chicago within two months—from a different angle.

Let's consider it from Angela's point of view. How will she accurately decide what office space to lease? She has a tight time-frame of less than two months, and she needs to make a good decision quickly since the company can't afford to have her fly back to Chicago every time a new leasing opportunity comes up.

ANGELA'S DECISION MAKING

The matter looks much different from Angela's point of view than from John's.

John tells Angela that he's putting her in charge of finding new office space in Chicago within two months. She has a lot of decisions to make, and fast. How does she handle it?

John knows that Angela has been trained in the same easy system that I'm sharing with you today. He is confident that she'll handle all the decisions very well, and accurately.

Let's see how she does it.

1. PURPOSE

First, Angela asks John what his purpose is in expanding the office to Chicago. This will help her immensely in her search. It will give her clear focus. It will help her define criteria and nonnegotiables.

John responds: "Angela, we want to open new customer service and sales departments in the Midwest. This will enable us to be more responsive to a growing segment of our business in the Midwestern region."

Perfect. Now Angela knows the purpose of the Chicago expansion: To better serve and expand the company's Midwestern client base by opening Midwest (Chicago) customer service and sales departments.

She advances to the next step in good decision making.

2. CRITERIA: NONNEGOTIABLES

Angela next asks John if there are any nonnegotiable or must-have criteria? Are there any "desirable, but not critical" criteria?

John is ready for this question. He hands Angela the same folder that had been given to him by the VP in charge of business development. In the folder, Angela finds the VP's notes.

John has also read through the folder, and has spoken to the VP directly. He summarizes for Angela:

"Ideally, we're looking for a place near Lake Michigan, one with a bit of Chicago character since you know how the VP loves Chicago."

John continues, "We want the office fully functional in three months. We're looking for a long-term lease that won't cost more than $250,000 rent in the first year and won't increase in rent by more than 10 percent annually. We'll also want to satisfy the needs of our customer service and sales personnel so that they perform their jobs well. That about sums up the discussions I've had with the VP. Start tomorrow and give me an update every Friday."

Angela gets right to work.

She took notes in her iPad and now makes a list of all the criteria she's gathered so far, highlighting the nonnegotiable must haves.

DO IT:

Before we go further, I'd like you to write down all of Angela's critera that you think are nonnegotiable:

Let's see how you did.

HOW DO YOU KNOW IF IT'S NONNEGOTIABLE?

People can get hung up on the difference between nonnegotiable and negotiable criteria. Sometimes the nonnegotiables jump out at you. For example, these two items from Angela's criteria are clearly nonnegotiable:

1. Not more than $250,000 rent

2. Maximum rent increase 10 percent annually

It's almost instinctive. But you know we can't rely on instinct alone! You could never justify choices that were based on instinct alone to a superior at work or to anyone else. And, instinct is not foolproof.

So here are the two secret components to determine whether or not a criterion is nonnegotiable:

1. **Can't-live-without it**. Is the criterion something that you seriously must have? Is it essential to your purpose?

2. **Measurable**. Is the criterion objectively measurable (not subject to someone's opinion)? The litmus test on "objectively measurable" is whether you can compare your options to this criterion and determine an immediate yes or no answer—without any discussion, interpretation, or opinion. If so, then this "can't-live-without it" item is a nonnegotiable.

Let's see if it works.

- *Not more than $250,000 rent*—Yes, this is measurable. It's black and white, as they say. An option will either meet this criterion or not. No opinion or interpretation needed.

- *Maximum rent increase 10 percent annually*—Yes again. This is measurable. Any comparison will either meet this criterion or not. No discussion or opinion needed.

Now, let's consider another criterion of Angela's:

- Long-term lease

Did you include long-term lease in your nonnegotiable criteria? Many do. It's tricky if you don't know the secret to determine which are nonnegotiables.

Consider it again.

Can various options be compared to long-term lease and generate a clear yes or no response, without opinion, discussion, or interpretation? No! You would have to assume what the VP considered to be long-term. Would it be six months? One year? Three years or more?

See what I mean? You can't compare various options to long-term lease and get an immediate, objective yes or no response.

Angela could ask John to clarify what he meant by long-term lease, then—and only then—she would have a measurable criterion. But Angela chooses not to ask her boss this question. Therefore, long-term lease is not a nonnegotiable.

DON'T CONFUSE "HIGHLY DESIRABLE" WITH "NONNEGOTIABLE"

I've also noticed that sometimes people confuse must-have nonnegotiables with highly desirable, but negotiable, criteria.

There's an easy way to determine whether something is nonnegotiable. Ask whether the decision could go forward if this item were not met. What would the results be? If lacking a specific criterion would cause a decision to fail, then you can be certain this is a nonnegotiable. But if the decision could go forward in spite of not meeting a certain criterion, no matter how desirable it is, then it does not qualify as a nonnegotiable.

It's critical in good decision making to be strict about what is nonnegotiable.

Consider Angela's criterion factor "Move-in ready in three months," for example. At first blush, you might consider it a nonnegotiable. It's certainly important. But think about it. If Angela came back to John with a $400,000 rent proposal—no way! That offer would be off the table in a nanosecond.

But if Angela came back to John with a four-month timeline, and if all else measured up, he'd probably accommodate the new move-in timeline. That makes the upper rent limit of $250,000 a nonnegotiable criterion, and it makes "Move-in ready in three months" negotiable, even though it is still highly desirable. A move-in date that was seven months out might be a deal breaker, but a timeline of four months is probably negotiable.

After the meeting with John, Angela's list looks like this:

PURPOSE:

To better serve and expand the company's Midwestern client base by opening Midwest (Chicago) Customer Service and Sales departments.

CRITERIA:

Move-in ready in three months

Chicago "character"

Near Lake Michigan

Maximum rent $250,000 first year

Long-term lease

Maximum 10 percent rent increase annually

Unknown: Sales & Customer Service personnel needs

Unknown: Square footage needed

Angela makes flight, car rental, and hotel arrangements for her trip to Chicago. She'll leave next week. She wants to make sure she has time to get the answers to her "unknown" criteria. She also wants to set up a few meetings with some Chicago commercial real estate brokers before she leaves.

Next, Angela talks with the heads of Customer Service and Sales regarding their plans for the expansion. She also sets up time to interview several of the top sales professionals, to learn their office needs for good performance and morale.

Customer Service will start with eight employees and Sales will bring a sales force of five, plus other personnel—assistants, office manager, and sales and customer service support. Nearby parking is important for the sales reps, who will need to leave at a moment's notice or to have prospective clients meet at the office. Good restaurants within walking distance were requested by all.

Also, a few things will be different from the home office. Because the company values a progressive approach to the workplace and building employee morale, the Customer Service and Sales anticipate that one-third of the Chicago employees will work mostly from home and will come into the office only for meetings or brainstorming, or because they feel a need to do so.

This flex work arrangement requires flexible work areas or zones that can be used for large or small intimate meetings, and other zones where the at-home staff can have access to a desk, computer, phone, and basics. The VP's folder notes indicate wanting to branch out more in the domain of cutting-edge office layout as well, which calls for greater flexibility in the work space altogether. That means less overall square footage will be needed than for a traditional, cubicle-based office layout. It also means no need for big corner offices or separate rooms, yet there must be enough separation and sound management so that the constant phone dialogue of customer service won't distract sales efforts, and so that meetings can be private if needed.

Angela consulted with the company's HR and Facility Management departments, which determined she needed to find a minimum of 8,000 square feet for office space.

Appointments with commercial real estate brokers are made. She's ready to board the plane to Chicago. Angela's list now looks like this:

PURPOSE:

To better serve and expand the company's Midwestern client base by opening Midwest (Chicago) Customer Service and Sales departments.

CRITERIA:

Move-in ready in three months

Chicago "character"

Near Lake Michigan

Maximum rent $250,000 first year

Long-term lease

Maximum 10 percent rent increase annually

Good restaurants nearby

Open space for flexible layout

Minimum 8,000 square feet

Nearby parking

On Angela's list, the Nonnegotiable must-haves are clear. She can immediately compare any option to these and get a yes or no answer without further thought:

Maximum rent $250,000 first year

Maximum 10 percent rent increase annually

Minimum 8,000 square feet

Now she needs greater clarity about the desirable, negotiable criteria.

APPLY THE 1–10 SCALE

Are certain negotiable items more desirable than others? Yes! As we've just seen, for example, move-in ready in three months is somewhat negotiable but it's still very important, more important than having a location near Lake Michigan or having Chicago character.

So, how do we determine which desirable is most important, and which is least?

I've found that the 1–10 scale works best and is easiest. This is the same system we used to determine priorities in an earlier chapter. 1 is the least important and 10 the most important.

Angela looks over her list of negotiables. She first identifies the most important, the most desirable, compared to everything else on the list. That gets a 10. She gives a 10 to "Move-in ready in three months."

Now she looks at each of the other negotiable criteria and asks herself: How does this item compare to "Move-in ready in three months"? Is it just a little less negotiable, or is it way down on the list? She assigns that item a low or high number depending on her answer to the question.

It's important to know what your top desirable criteria are. These may be needed to serve as a tiebreaker if two options are very similar, as you'll see later on.

3. COMPARE OPTIONS TO CRITERIA, NOT TO EACH OTHER

Upon arriving in Chicago, Angela decides which broker she'll work with and shows him her criteria for office space. He finds several options that he thinks will work for her. Here's the important point: Angela must consider each option *in relation to her criteria.*

Decision makers can get stuck on this point. I've seen people agonizing over various options, repeatedly comparing one option to another option. It's an endless cycle in frustration. The secret is not to compare one option to another, but instead to compare each option to the criteria.

Let's see how Angela performs.

The broker shows Angela several locations.

She has no trouble eliminating a few options immediately. The first, located near Lake Shore Drive, seems ideal, dripping with Chicago "character." But when she learns the rent is $400,000 the first year, way beyond the VP's maximum, it is no longer an option. Other locations met the price requirement but were in such sketchy areas that no one would feel safe walking to a restaurant or even parking their car. Easy elimination. The broker then shows her three reasonable possibilities.

Her options look like this:

- **Option 1: Michigan Avenue**

  Just north of the Loop, the 9,000-square-foot site rents for $250,000 a year, pushing up against the VP's maximum price allotment. A five-year lease is available, with annual rent increase of 6 percent a year. The building is an historic landmark in Chicago. Parking isn't the best at this location, but the nearby restaurants are first-rate. The eastward-facing office has a wonderful view of the lake, which would surely make the VP happy.

- **Option 2: Grand Avenue**

  This location is in a brick building with a little more space than the criterion, 10,000 square feet. Rent is less expensive at only $180,500 a year, but the building is being refurbished and might not be available within three months. Parking is plentiful and easy to access, yet a hot dog kiosk on the next block is the closest thing to a nearby restaurant. Rent increase on the space is 7 percent a year.

- **Option 3: LaSalle Street**

  As soon as the broker opens the door, Angela feels good about the place. It's bright, with a lot of natural light. The building exterior and the room's crown molding give it a subtle hint of Chicago character. She knows employees will feel good working here. This was the smallest of the three viable options, at 8,000 square feet. This location is also the most costly, at $300,000 the first year, just slightly above the maximum rent desired. Rent increases will be 10 percent annually. Nice restaurants and trees line the street. The higher price reflects its superb location near the heart of the financial district.

All three options allow for flexible layout. Asking further questions, Angela learns that the Michigan Avenue and LaSalle Street places are available immediately. She also found out that the LaSalle Street and Grand Avenue locations have a three-year lease option.

What to do? Angela was torn. She had to make some tough decisions. She fell in love with the LaSalle Street location at first sight. It was clearly the nicest option of the three, but she couldn't fall prey to her personal preferences. She must follow the decision-making process. She knows that she has to *delete any options that don't meet nonnegotiables.*

Angela looks over her options again, and immediately eliminates Option 3 (LaSalle Street) because it does not meet her nonnegotiable criteria.

"But LaSalle Street was Angela's favorite option!" you say. And you're right. But in Option 3 (LaSalle Street) the rent exceeded the nonnegotiable of $250,000/year. Everything else about this location is irrelevant, even her initial attraction to it.

This is so important: Angela immediately eliminated the very location that she liked the best because it did not meet nonnegotiable criteria. Done. Simple. Off the table.

We've all seen people agonize over options that were way out of their price range, or that were something they could not ultimately live with, just because they were emotionally drawn to it.

It's kind of like falling in love with the wrong guy or girl— someone who's clearly an in-denial alcoholic or who doesn't want children and you do. The person is loving and a lot of fun. But you can't live with that person without twisting yourself into a pretzel.

Remember, you want to make good, accurate decisions every time. So it's important to carefully choose objective yes or no nonnegotiables and go through the process. It's the only way to end up with a winning, good decision every time.

That was easy!

How do Angela's remaining two options measure up to the criteria?

Both Options 1 and 2 satisfy the nonnegotiables. But looking at the negotiable criteria, Angela sees that there are pros and cons for each option.

She's most concerned with the highest-ranked negotiable criterion. Option 1 (Michigan Avenue) meets her highest negotiable, which is a three-month move-in date. But it doesn't meet her second-highest negotiable, easy access to nearby parking.

On the other hand, Option 2 (Grand Avenue) meets the parking criterion, but Angela is not sure if the refurbishing will be completed within three months. Other negotiable criteria are ranked lower.

Some people like to see everything laid out on paper or on a computer screen. Sometimes to see it this way gives you an immediate sense of the whole picture.

To make it easy, I listed all of the nonnegotiable and negotiable criteria for Angela's remaining two options. As you can see, there's a check mark ☑ beside elements that matched her criteria, and an ☒ by those that didn't.

Remember, options are only compared to the criteria.

Options are not compared to each other yet.

Here's a quick look at Angela's remaining two options and how they compare to her criteria.

Angela's quick list comparing Option 1 and 2 to the Criteria:

CRITERIA

NONNEGOTIABLE

Max. rent $250,000 first year

Max. 10% rent increase per year

Min. 8,000 square feet

NEGOTIABLE

⑩ Move-in ready in three months

⑧ Nearby parking

⑦ Long-term lease

⑥ Good restaurants nearby

⑤ Flexible space

④ Near Lake Michigan

③ Chicago "character"

OPTION 1: Michigan Avenue

Compare to Criteria:

NONNEGOTIABLE

☑ $250,000 first year

☑ Rent increase of 6% a year

☑ 9,000 square feet

NEGOTIABLE

☑ Available now

☒ Parking not the best

☑ Five-year lease available

☑ Nearby restaurants first-rate

☑ Flexible space

☑ View of Lake Michigan

☑ Historic landmark

OPTION 2: Grand Avenue

Compare to Criteria

NONNEGOTIABLE

☑ 180,500 first year

☑ Rent increase of 7% a year

☑ 10,000 square feet

NEGOTIABLE

☒ Unsure of move-in date

☑ Parking plentiful & easy

☑ Three-year lease

☒ Hot dog stand, no restaurants

☑ Flexible space

☑ Not too far from lake

☑ Brick building

At this point, Angela is inclined to choose Option 1 (Michigan Avenue) because it is the only remaining option that includes Angela's highest-rated negotiable criterion ("Move-in ready in three months"). But her decision making is not yet complete. She must identify and assess risks associated with each option before being confident of making a good, accurate decision.

4. IDENTIFY AND ASSESS RISKS

This is a critical step. Neither of Angela's remaining two locations measure up to her criteria perfectly. That's the case with most options. Nothing is perfect. Identifying and assessing risks allows Angela to make the best decision given the factors she knows at the time of the decision.

In this step, Angela not only identifies the risks associated with each remaining option, she also assesses whether she can live with any risk she identifies.

Again, just like a good coach who trains his players to anticipate opponent strategies and attacks, Angela won't leave herself—or her VP—blindsided by problems down the road. She identifies and assesses risks for each option now, ahead of time.

To identify risks, Angela looks for missing criteria and for barely met criteria in each option she is considering.

For each option, Angela asks herself: "What might happen if I choose this option, with these missing or barely met criteria? What might happen if things don't go exactly as anticipated— will the missing or barely met criteria cause the decision to fail?" This is especially important if it is a barely met, non-negotiatable criteria.

It's easy. Identify a risk by asking, for each missing or barely met criterion: What's the worst reasonable thing that could happen?

To assess a risk once it's identified, Angela must determine whether she can (or can't) live with it. She must decide whether she can (or can't) manage that risk. And she must know how serious it is. A missing or barely met criterion would be more serious, for example, if it were a highly ranked negotiable.

Put simply, a risk is assessed by asking:

Can I live with this risk?

Can I manage this risk?

How serious is it?

Now Angela is ready to identify and assess risks associated with each of her remaining options. Let's see how she does.

IDENTIFY THE RISKS

Angela first identifies risks associated with Option 1 (Michigan Avenue). The only criterion not met by this option is "easily accessible nearby parking."

But Angela notices that there is also a barely met criterion. She is concerned that the rent is right at her $250,000 maximum limit. Even though this cost meets her criterion, it is at the uppermost limit. Any downturn in company revenue could cause problems, so she adds this as a potential risk.

That was easy!

Angela identifies her risks for Option 1 (Michigan Avenue) like this:

- **Option 1: Michigan Avenue Risks**

  Missing criterion: Easily accessible nearby parking

  What is the worst reasonable thing that could happen?

  - Employees may arrive late and frustrated for work or meetings.

  - Clients may not want to visit the office.

  Barely met criteria: Maximum rent $250,000 the first year

  What is the worst reasonable thing that could happen?

  - An unexpected downturn in revenue could put the company in the red.

Angela identifies her risks for Option 2 (Grand Avenue) like this:

- **Option 2: Grand Avenue Risks**

  Missing criterion: Office space might not be available in three months.

  What is the worst reasonable thing that could happen?

  - The revenue contribution anticipated by the VP from the new Chicago office might not be met.

ASSESS THE RISKS

There's no need to get complicated and conflicted at this point. Every decision involves some risk. Every option involves some benefits and some conflicts.

Take another look at the risks you have identified. Which risks can you live with, or manage? Which risks are intolerable? How serious are these risks?

For Angela, the risk identification and assessment process does not affect her tentative choice for Option 1, the Michigan Avenue location. Instead, this process only confirmed that Option 1 was the right choice.

Let me explain.

The highest-ranked (10) negotiable on Angela's list is "move-in ready in three months." Because this is the highest ranking negotiable on Angela's list, it is the most important among all the negotiables. Therefore if this criterion is missing from an option, the consequences are bigger and more severe than if other criteria are missing.

In the risk identification process, Angela saw that the highest-ranked criterion ("move-in ready in three months") is missing in Option 2, the Grand Avenue location. She saw that this could result in loss of income for the company. Not good.

As she looks over the risks associated with Option 1, Michigan Avenue ("employees arriving late or frustrated to the office" and "customers not wanting to visit the office"), Angela sees clearly that these are much less consequential than the risk associated with not being move-in ready in three months. Though not desirable, Angela can manage these risks. They are not a deal breaker for her.

But remember, Angela also identified a barely met risk with Option 1.

Option 1 (Michigan Avenue) is at the highest limit of rent allowance. This poses some risk, as Angela has identified. But Angela realizes that the VP has certainly given her a carefully calculated rent price and she is not exceeding it. So, this risk is nearly moot. She can live with it.

Angela makes her final decision. She chooses Option 1, the Michigan Avenue location, for the new Chicago office.

That's it. Done.

Angela returns to the home office with a clear decision and a signed contract for Option 1, the Michigan Avenue office space.

When John asks for her reasoning, Angela is able to present her decision-making process succinctly and clearly. He's delighted with the results and passes the good news to the VP.

DO IT:

Fill out the following guides (or use a separate piece of paper, your iPad, or computer) to make a decision about your Dump List concerns that you've fast-tracked as needing the decision-making skill to resolve.

- State the Decision You Have to Make (from Dump List. Choose one of your "Decide now" concerns):

- Purpose of Decision:

- List Your Criteria:

- In the Previous List, Highlight or Circle All Your Nonnegotiables. Remember to be very strict about this. An option must be able to be compared to a nonnegotiable and get an immediate, clear yes or no answer.

- In the Previous List, Rank Your Desireable or Negotiable Criteria. Rank These From 1–10 (1 is least desirable and 10 is most desirable. Choose which negotiable is a 10, then compare everything else in importance to this 10.)

- How Does Each of Your Options Compare to Your Nonnegotiable Criteria?

- What Options Did You Immediately Eliminate Because They Did Not Meet Your Nonnegotiables?

- How Does Each of Your Remaining Options Compare to Your Desirables or Negotiables?

- Which Option Do You Tentatively Choose? Remember, this option will have the most high-ranking desirables, ideally including the highest ranked.

- Identify and Assess Risk: Remember, for your tentative choice and the next-closest option, ask: What could go wrong if I choose this option? Then assess your answers by asking: Could I live with it? Could I manage it? How serious is it? Write your answers:

• What is Your Final Decision?

You did it!

You just eliminated one of your Dump List concerns that required the decision-making skill. Congratulations!

See how easy this is?

Here is a simple reminder to keep you focused in future decision-making concerns.

REMEMBER:

- Consistent, good decision making requires all of these four steps:

  1. DEFINE PURPOSE: What's the purpose of the decision?

  2. ESTABLISH CRITERIA: What are the negotiable and nonnegotiable factors?

  3. COMPARE OPTIONS TO CRITERIA: How does each option measure up?

  4. ASSESS RISKS: What are the risks—and how serious—associated with each option?

  DECIDE NOW!

Chapter Eight

PAST: FIND OUT "WHY?"

Never ignore a gut feeling, but never believe that it's enough.

—Robert Heller

The second most common thinking skill we use on a daily basis is often called problem solving. In this skill, we need to find out why something happened, or what went wrong (or what went right!). It always involves looking back to the past and evaluating.

"Well, that's no big deal. I do that every day," you say. And so you do.

But, is it your habit to over- or under analyze a problem? Do you tend to hit the mark all the time, or is it hit or miss? What if it's a complicated issue? Could you justify your reasoning process if someone asked you to do so? Most importantly, are you confident that you'll come up with a clear and accurate answer *every* time?

The good news is: I'm confident that I can teach you an easy system to "find out why" accurately, every time.

So let's get started.

Here are the basic problem-solving steps we'll learn in this chapter:

1. State the problem
2. Gather facts
3. Compare
4. Look for differences/changes
5. Verify likely cause

1. STATE THE PROBLEM

As you might have noticed, every solution to our Dump List concerns begins with a clear statement that gives us laser like focus on the task at hand. In the skill of problem solving, we're like detectives figuring out "who done it?" Whether we're trying to find out what our company did to generate off-the-charts sales last quarter, or why our teammate who plays first base keeps missing the ball, our first step in finding answers is a clear statement about what we're looking for.

Pulling from John's Dump List, how would each of his "find out why" concerns be rewritten as clear statements to tell us what we're looking for?

JOHN'S "FIND OUT WHY" CONCERNS	STATE THE PROBLEM
Talk with HR to learn why reduction plan is behind schedule.	← Find out why the reduction plan is behind schedule.

Find out why sales and marketing employees have poor morale.	← Find out why sales and marketing employees have poor morale.
Find out cause of dying trees on farms near Midwest plant.	← Find out cause of dying trees on farms near Midwest plant.
Find out details on airline space limitations.	← Find out why the wine bottles cause problems for the airline.

DO IT:

Now list your own "find out why" concerns, pulled from your Dump List. Next to each concern, create a clear statement to give you focus in your search.

LIST YOUR "FIND OUT WHY" CONCERNS	STATE THE PROBLEM
	←
	←
	←
	←

Great work! Now you're "cookin' with gas," as my father used to say!

The next step in problem solving is to gather the facts.

2. GATHER THE FACTS

This step is as simple as it sounds. Just like a detective or a news reporter on the scene of breaking news or a crime, you're going to "gather the facts"—*only the important facts*—surrounding the issue you're trying to resolve.

Beware: Don't *assume* anything! This is important to remember.

Sometimes things seem obvious to us, so we just assume that what we think is true. But it's not always the case, and we have no way of knowing—at this first step of problem solving—whether our assumption is correct.

For example, we see a child not turn in his homework week after week and we might assume he's lazy. But the truth might be that he has to help out with the family business every night after he gets home from school and his parents don't allow him time to do homework. Or, maybe he suffers from a reading disability that makes understanding his homework impossible. Our initial assumption might be correct, or it might be incorrect. We don't know yet. We would miss finding out the truth if we just stopped at our assumptions.

"But how will I know the important facts about something?" you cry out. Not to worry. I have an easy system that has helped thousands of people just like you figure out why something happened with ease and accuracy, every time!

Here's the secret to gathering the important facts: Just like a detective, ask "What?" "Where?" "When?" "How many?" "How much?" "What's the trend?"

Let's consider one of John's "find out why" concerns:

Find out cause of dying trees on farms near Midwest plant.

To give you a little insider background on this issue, farmers first started noticing a few trees dying in their cherry orchards about two years ago. They thought it was odd, talked a little about it with other farmers, and did some minor insect and blight investigation. Nothing explained the problem. They didn't think much more about it until last year when they noticed more trees dying. This year the number was greater and farmers were starting to point fingers at the company's Midwest plant. John needed to find out the cause of those dying trees to determine if their plant has anything to do with the farmer's plight.

Statement

The first thing John does is clarify his search with a statement: Find out why trees are dying on farms near the Midwest plant.

Gather Facts with Questions

Next, just as a detective would do, John gathers only the important facts by asking the following questions:

What? John needs to know what the problem is, or what it is that he wants to repeat. For example, is something defective? Has something gone wrong? Do good results need to be duplicated? The answer must be a clear statement. Here's how John answers the question "What?"

Cherry trees are dying on farms near the Midwest plant.

Where? This is a good question. Many facts can be gathered with this question. John does some investigation and interviews and finds out these answers:

The only farms affected are those downstream from the plant.

The only trees dying are located closer to the river.

When? This is one of the most revealing questions of all. When does the problem—or good thing—occur? Or, when did it start? John writes down what he learns:

Farmers began noticing dying trees two years ago.

First reports came in during the early Fall, in September.

How much? How many? What is the trend? It's important to know what the trend is. For example, is a problem getting better or worse? Is the number of affected farms increasing or decreasing? John writes down what he knows:

The trend is increasing. Each year the problem gets worse.

DO IT:

Now pick one of your "Find Out Why" concerns, use the statement you already wrote earlier, and follow through the initial "Gather the Facts" process using the simple, easy-to-use questions.

Remember, you're acting like a detective, so write down as many answers to the critical questions as you can. Feel free to get more information from other people if needed. After all, you're gathering the facts!

What? What is happening that is defective or wrong, or in some cases, what is right so it can be repeated?

Where? Where does it happen?

When? When does the problem—or good thing—occur? And when did it start?

How much? How many? What is the trend?

Great job!

Now you must compare these facts with other facts. This is a critical step in digging down to understand why something happens.

Let me explain.

3. COMPARE

Fact gathering includes comparison with other facts. This enables you to see your focused issue within a wider context. Remember, you're trying to find out the cause for something. You're asking "Why does (or did) this happen?" The answer—or at least a good clue—might pop out at you when you compare your facts to those of other, similar situations.

Consider a detective.

In a murder investigation the detective not only gathers important facts and evidence at the crime scene. He also sifts these facts against other facts. He compares them. He looks for something different, something that feels off, or out of the ordinary. He also does a comparison and sifting of facts when he interviews different suspects and witnesses, when he checks alibis and the accounts that different people give about the event.

For example, let's say that one of the suspects gives an alibi. She says she was at a concert on the night of the crime. She was with her boyfriend. Okay. That's an important fact because it might eliminate this suspect. But the detective doesn't stop with this fact.

The detective compares the important fact with other facts. In this example, he tracks down the boyfriend. The boyfriend confirms that he was with the suspect at the concert on the night of the crime. So far, the suspect's alibi checks out.

But the detective doesn't stop there. He compares more facts. The detective looks up the concert date. Was that concert actually performed on the date in question? Aha! He learns that there was no concert on that date! The concert was the day before the crime. So, both the suspect and the boyfriend aren't telling the truth. What are they hiding? Did one or both commit the crime?

The detective continues to compare important facts with other facts. He follows a process that works, time and time again. We do the same.

You can see how comparing your situation with other facts will give you a bigger perspective. You can see how you might discover clues to the right answer by sifting and comparing facts.

4. PAY ATTENTION TO DIFFERENCES/CHANGES

Like a detective, you also must pay attention to any differences and/or changes in the fact-gathering phase.

For example, let's say that the murder victim had the habit of always saying "Hey, how's it going?" to the security guard at the front desk of his condo high-rise every time he passed by. For three years, the murder victim never failed to make this friendly comment.

But on the night of the murder, the security guard distinctly remembers that the victim rushed by without delivering a greeting. The guard thought it was odd, but didn't think much about it until he learned about the murder. It seemed insignificant, but he mentioned it to the detective anyway.

For the detective it was a clue. It was a change from the norm. As it turned out, this little clue gave credence to another person's observation that the murder victim seemed unusually distraught that same morning. Had he fought with someone? Did he learn something horrific? Was he being threatened or blackmailed for some reason? The point is that paying attention to differences and changes is what delivered the clues.

In another example, let's say that a radical change of temperature in manufacturing affects a product's functionality. But no one realizes this until a manufacturing company in Florida, which has near tropical weather, opens a manufacturing plant in Michigan, which has severe winters. The manufacturing equipment and process are exactly the same in both locations, but six months into operation, the company starts getting complaints that products aren't working correctly. The company tracks down the defective products and learns that they are only coming from the Michigan plant.

They further compare, and pay attention to changes, and learn that these defective products were manufactured from January to March in the Michigan plant and shipped out immediately. Comparison to the products from the Florida plant and paying attention to, in this case, dramatic weather differences between the two plants at the time of production leads the company to figure out that early exposure to extreme cold is the cause of their defective production.

Very Important: Look Again

I've noticed that many people do not at first understand how important it is to look for what is different or changed. Some think they understand this step, but it is clear that they do not. This experience is so common that we find it almost predictable in every class we teach.

You see, *looking for differences or changes will have more significant impact on your problem-solving skills than any other consideration.* This is true whether you are an entrepreneur, a waiter, a doctor, a detective, or a CEO.

What's really exciting for me is to finally see the "*Now* I get it!" lightbulb of understanding on the individual faces and in the eyes of the tens of thousands of people who have learned this system.

Once this lightbulb goes on, you will become virtually unstoppable in your ability to solve problems or get to the bottom of results that you want to repeat.

That's why I encourage you to look at this again.

As an example, let's look at professionals from two very different fields: a doctor and a detective. Do you realize that a doctor and a detective have a lot in common? Surprising, isn't it? Yet true.

A doctor must diagnose an illness. A detective must diagnose a crime. In both cases, the process is exactly the same.

"You're kidding!" you say. Nope! Not only do they use the same process, they use it again and again. It works. And it will work for you too, just as it works for them.

Look for *differences* and *changes*.

Let me explain.

Consider the doctor. A patient with what seems to be a serious disease comes in to see him. The doctor checks the patient for his symptoms, he takes blood pressure, and so forth. One of the first questions a doctor asks the patient is this: Is there anyone else who has the same symptoms?

With this question the doctor is trying to see if the patient is different from other people. He is trying to isolate the patient from the total population to see if he is the only case, or if there are other people who have the same illness. If there are other people who have the same illness, then maybe the doctor will be able to identify a pattern and get to the cause.

Those with the illness are different from the norm. The norm in this case is the vast remainder of the population who *could* have contracted the same disease but did not.

The doctor knows what (or, in this case, who) is different. He also knows the norm. Now he is ready to move to the next step in diagnosing the patient's illness.

Next, the doctor seeks to find out what has changed with the patient. He asks:

Has the patient done anything out of the ordinary recently?

Has the patient traveled to any foreign country recently?

Has he eaten anything new or unusual?

Has the patient introduced anything new into his system?

If a patient comes in with symptoms that include a rapidly spreading rash, for example, and tells the doctor that he started taking new vitamins two weeks earlier, this is a clear change from the norm for this patient. So the doctor suspects that this patient does not have a horrible disease, but rather that he is allergic to something in the new vitamins. The doctor orders the patient to stop taking the new vitamins. He wants to see if the rash will clear up. If so, problem solved!

If the patient is cured of his symptoms when he stops taking the vitamins, the clue that led the doctor to solve the patient's problem is a change. In this example, what changed is that the patient began taking new vitamins.

However, if there are other people who have the same illness and rash, yet who do not take the vitamins, then the doctor knows the vitamins are not the cause of the problem.

Okay. What about a detective?

Same process. A detective looks for differences and changes.

In a murder crime, the detective wants to find out who has motive to commit the crime. A person who has a motive is *different* from everyone else. Once a detective finds out who is different, then he can go to the next step.

Next, the detective will investigate whether there is anything in the person's life that has changed, possibly causing him to want to murder the victim.

For example, a detective notices that the son of a wealthy businessman has come into desperate financial times. The son has always been the heir to the businessman's fortune, but something must have changed in his life to make him want to murder his father and collect his inheritance sooner rather than later. Maybe this suspect had a thriving business that went bust five months earlier when its largest client suddenly cancelled all orders and declared bankruptcy. This suspect was left holding not only an enormous debt, but also customized products that could not be sold even at cost. Worse, the son had not managed the business well and relied too heavily on this one client for his cash flow. When he approached his father in desperation, his father had flatly refused financial assistance and had even ridiculed the son's decisions. Furious and too ashamed to go elsewhere to assuage his dire financial straits, perhaps he turned to murder.

But that's not all.

The detective notices that another suspect has undergone a dramatic change in his life that may have driven him to murder as well. This second suspect gambled away all his money last month and now owes $30,000 that he'd borrowed from a shady gambling buddy.

You know how the story goes.

"I'll pay it back in a month," the suspect promises. But he can't honor his promise—his mortgage is due. His daughter is getting married. He just lost his job as partner in a big law firm. Now what? The shady character who loaned this suspect $30K told him he'd better pay up or harm will come to the gambler's family. The gambler was the murder victim's lawyer. And as his lawyer, he was privy to how much money the victim possessed. Would the gambler have motive to murder the victim? Yes. Would the son? Yes. Could they have done it together? Maybe.

Who committed the crime? That's a different question. The detective doesn't know the answer yet. All the detective is looking for at this point is to identify "Which suspects have motive?" and "What changed in their lives to possibly cause them to commit a murder?"

What led the detective to determine whether or not this suspect had motive? Like the doctor in the earlier example, the detective is relentlessly focused only on finding out who is different from the rest of the population and what has changed in each suspect's life. In this case, both the son and the gambler lawyer had a significant change in their financial circumstances and the murder victim was very wealthy. Looking for change and difference led the detective to discover that two suspects had motive.

Both the doctor and the detective look for what is different and changed.

You must do the same!

One More Example

Here is just one more example, a very easy and common one.

Imagine that you and five friends have lunch. The next day, one friend asks if you got violently sick the night before. You say no. But your friend did become violently ill. She wonders if she experienced food poisoning.

How will you two figure it out?

You will try to determine if she ate something different from everyone else.

Hmmm. You remember the meals of each person at the lunch. You all had the same soft drink. You all shared in the same dessert. You all had soup and salad. But your friend who became ill is the only one who ate fish. Everyone else ordered chicken.

What is different? Your friend is the only one who ordered fish at the restaurant. Fish is the only thing different. You both suspect that this is what caused your friend's sudden and violent illness that same evening.

You go further in this investigation to find out what has changed. You and your friend could explain the situation to the restaurant owner. The owner could research what changed about the fish meal served on that particular day. After all, the owner has been in business for 13 years and no one complained about the fish like this before. What changed? Maybe the owner discovers that the head chef purchased fish from a new vendor on that day. That is a change. Further investigation reveals that two other fish meals served on that day were sent back because they "tasted funny."

The head chef had not used his normal fish vendor because the vendor's prices had increased and that affected the chef's bottom line. But now the restaurant owner has solid reason to suspect that the cause of your friend's illness was indeed the fish, the fish from one specific rogue vendor.

See how easy it is to find out the cause of something by looking for differences and changes!

In more complex situations, such as figuring out the cause of manufacturing defects or the cause of a stock market rally, the important thing to remember is to look for differences and changes.

Doggedly, persistently search for what is different and what has changed. Do not get sidetracked. Looking for differences and changes works every time when you want to find out the "why" of something.

Let's see how John does.

When John spoke earlier with the Midwest plant engineer, he learned that this plant was relatively new. It opened in March two years ago. John also learned that the company introduced a new manufacturing process at this plant, which involved using several new chemicals not previously used in other plants. He also learned from the affected farmers that they had paid agricultural experts to test the trees on different farms for insects or blight. Nothing came up positive.

John compares these facts with his original facts, and sifts through them, looking for differences and changes. He writes down his discoveries.

COMPARE:

- Trees on farms upstream of the plant (no problem).
- Trees located inland from the river, in the same orchard as dying trees (no problem).

- Trees downstream before the plant was operational (no problem).

- Trees downstream by the river after the plant was built (dying two years ago, six months after new plant became operational).

- Trees located downstream are dying in bigger numbers each year (trend is increasing).

Having now gathered all the important facts he can find, and having compared them with other similar situations or products, and having paid attention to any changes or differences between them, John sits back and looks at what he's uncovered.

A Tentative Answer

Based on the comparisons and noting any differences or changes, John comes up with a tentative answer to his search:

The trees are most likely dying because of chemicals in the water from the new plant, which became operational six months before the trees began to die.

He now must verify his answer.

But before we proceed . . .

DO IT:

Now compare your situations or products with similar situations or products. Compare your initial facts to "before" and "after" times. Ask the questions: What? Where? When? How Much? How Many? What is the trend?

Be sure to note any differences or changes.

COMPARE:

_____

_____

_____

_____

_____

Now sit back. Relax. Get up and stretch. Take a short walk around the block. Look at how much progress you've made! I bet you feel like a real detective now.

You have all the facts and clues you can dig up at this point. So, what differences and changes do you notice? How do these observations and facts fit with the conversations you've had with others regarding the issue? How do they fit with whatever you are trying to determine (your statement)? What do you suspect is the answer to your statement?

My proposed conclusion is:

_____

_____

_____

Great job, sleuth! Now you must verify your proposed conclusion.

But before verifying your proposed conclusion, let's see what John did.

5. GENERATE AND VERIFY LIKELY CAUSE

You remember John's tentative conclusion:

- The trees are most likely dying because of chemicals in the water from the new plant, which became operational six months before the trees began to die.

Now John must verify his conclusion.

This is a critical step. He doesn't want to run on a hunch, not even an educated hunch. That could be a waste of time, energy, and resources. Instead, he must verify his proposed conclusion *before he does anything else!*

John picks up the phone and calls the Midwest plant. He wants a water test done as soon as possible in order to learn what chemicals, if any, are released into the water from the plant. For comparison, he wants the water tested upstream from the plant, as well as downstream.

If the water upstream does not reveal chemicals in the water, yet the downstream water tests positive for chemicals, then John will test further. He will then want to know if these chemicals could account for the dying trees.

The plant engineer jumps right on it. They'll be glad when this matter is resolved.

Fantastic!

John is feeling really good about his workload. Already he has eliminated more than half of the concerns on his simplified Dump List. Best of all, he's not stressed about anything. He is taking care of things in an organized way without feeling crazed or out of control, without feeling drained or zapped of energy. When he goes home at night, he has energy to give to his wife and children. Life has taken on a new sense of hope and fulfillment for him.

Regarding the dying trees, John is not yet positive he's found the cause of the problem. He won't know this until tests from engineering come in next week. But one thing he does know is that he's on the right track.

I don't want to leave you in suspense, so I'll let you know that engineering tests did confirm and verify John's proposed conclusion that chemical residue in the water, generated from the new plant, killed the trees near the water.

With the cause of the problem verified, John can now work on a solution. He'll assign engineering to work on finding a solution, and he'll ask the corporate legal department to put together several compensation offers to the farmers to minimize possible litigation. He'll then present these offers to the CFO for approval.

As simple as the solution might be from John's point of view, however, the engineering department will still have to conduct its own process to decide the best way to eliminate chemical residue from entering the river. But you know already that engineering will use the same decision-making process you've already learned. The same is true for the legal department. See how much progress you've made? Great job!

DO IT:

How will you verify the proposed conclusion to your concern? Write out your answer below:

I will verify my proposed conclusion in this way:

Was your proposed conclusion verified to be correct? If so, then you'll need to decide how to fix it, or assign someone else to do this.

Was your proposed conclusion not verified? Was it incorrect? If so, then go back over your comparisons. Note any differences and changes. Perhaps it would be helpful to enlist fresh eyes to go over this with you. Then, see if you can generate another proposed conclusion. Maybe you'll come up with a few more possibilities. Verify to see which is correct.

You've done a remarkable job!

You've made so much progress.

Now that you know the secret—the very simple, easy process for finding out why something occurred—you are well on your way to developing the valuable habit of accurately and consistently finding out the cause for issues whenever needed.

Just be sure to follow this easy, simple process and don't skip any steps.

Let's continue on.

REMEMBER:

- You have at your fingertips all the steps necessary to solve any query, to Find Out Why:

  1. State the problem

  2. Gather facts

  3. Compare

  4. Look for differences/changes

  5. Verify likely cause

  FIND OUT WHY

Chapter Nine

FUTURE:

PLAN TO MAKE IT HAPPEN

Some people want it to happen, some wish it would happen, others make it happen.

—Michael Jordan

There is no scarcity of opportunity to make a living at what you love; there's only scarcity of resolve to make it happen.

—Wayne Dyer

If you keep thinking about what you want to do or what you hope will happen, you don't do it, and it won't happen.

—Desiderius Erasmus

Have a bias toward action—let's see something happen now. You can break that big plan into small steps and take the first step right away.

—Indira Gandhi

You know better than anyone what it feels like to bring something to life; to make it happen. It's an amazing feeling, isn't it? It gives you confidence that you could do it again.

But if you are like I was before I developed this system with my colleagues, you also know what it's like to just about faint with joy whenever what you were planning actually did happen! Maybe some of your past achievements have been nearly miraculous in their results. Maybe your experience with planning and execution is less than stellar.

Maybe you know deep down that, honestly, your planning and execution have typically been a "hold on and hang on for the ride" experience. And maybe you also know deep down that you'll never advance or achieve your dreams with confidence if you don't do something different . . . and fast!

I offer you a simple way—a wonderfully easy way—to plan to make it happen.

Let's see how it works.

Remember when I asked you, at the very beginning of the book, to write down the names of several people whom you admired for their ability to stay calm and focused in any crisis? Think of those people again. How do they handle an unexpected change in plans? Do they fly off the handle in a rage? How do they handle last-minute urgencies? How do they make things happen?

Do these people you admire make things happen with a wing and a prayer, or do they seem to have a process, a system of execution? Have you ever wondered what their secret is? I'll let you in on that secret. The secret is next, in seven easy steps:

1. State the Objective

2. Develop an Action Plan

3. List Foreseeable Problems and Opportunities

4. Define How to Prevent or Facilitate

5. Define Back-Up ("Plan B")

6. Create Trigger Alerts

7. Update Your Action Plan

As with decision making and problem solving, Plan to Make it Happen starts with a statement of your objective. You know well by now that if you don't first know clearly where you are going, you will never know if you arrive! No objective; no achievement possible. It's as simple as that.

Let's see how this works.

1. STATE THE OBJECTIVE

Another way to express the term "objective" is "goal and purpose." What is the goal and purpose of the project at hand? Write it down, clearly and simply.

Be sure that all of these questions are answered in your statement: What do you want to accomplish? Where will it be accomplished? and When (by what date) will it be accomplished?

Anyone should be able to look at your stated objective and know immediately whether it was achieved.

As an example, let's take one of John's concerns:

• Plan French officials' visit by Friday.

No question. This is a high-pressure assignment. As you recall, John just returned from two weeks in Cancun. He has a full plate of new, demanding responsibilities. This added burden of planning a visit from top-tier foreign officials, in less than four days, would put most people over the top with anxiety.

John could have jumped with both feet into this one assignment, since it is clearly among the most urgent of his concerns. But he chose instead to Stop: Start Here: Stop and go through the process I'd taught him. He's glad he chose this route. Look at how much he's accomplished so far, and it's only the beginning of his second day at work!

Thanks to following the process, John is not panicked or anxious about planning the officials' visit. He feels good that some of his other concerns—more than half of them—were achieved or have begun to be addressed by the end of the day yesterday. He went home last night knowing that he'd tackle this planning assignment with a clear head the next morning, calmly and with confidence.

John trusts the same process you are learning here, and it works, every time.

Arriving to work fresh and rested, John looks at this concern. The first thing he must do in order to plan to make it happen is to state his objective.

John writes his objective like this:

- Objective: Plan the French officials' visit to our corporate office by this Friday.

You can see that John's objective statement answers all the questions regarding what he wants to accomplish, where it will be accomplished, and by when it will be accomplished.

What? "Plan the French officials' visit"

Where? "to our corporate office"

When? "by this Friday"

Great. That was easy.

2. DEVELOP AN ACTION PLAN

This is as easy as it sounds. Simply list all the steps you must accomplish in order to achieve your objective. Sometimes it will be a schedule of events. Sometimes it will look like a checklist. This is your action plan.

In John's case, the VP's assistant already created an event schedule for the French officials while John was still in Cancun. John must confirm it. He likes it and gives it his okay.

John's action plan looks like this:

SCHEDULED VISIT OF FRENCH OFFICIALS

Tuesday, April 24

1:30 p.m.	Arrival at SFO, Universal Flight #712 Press conference at VIP Lounge. Motorcade to hotel for check-in.
4:30 p.m.	Leave visitors to freshen up from trip.
5:45 p.m.	Travel by motorcade to private bayside club in Marin County.
8:30 p.m.	Evening cruise on San Francisco Bay, leaving from Tiburon pier.
11:15 p.m.	Return by limo to hotel.

Wednesday, April 25

7:30–11:30 a.m.	Golf at Twin Oaks Country Club with French-American celebrity.
1:00 p.m.	Tour of our corporate facilities (Manufacturing, Customer Support, Usability Lab, Selected Facilities). Includes buffet luncheon in executive suite and slide show in Board room.
6:00 p.m.	Reception and Dinner with San Francisco Mayor at the Top of the Mark.

Thursday, April 26

—	Morning free
1:00 p.m.	Poolside lunch at hotel.
	Afternoon tour bus to Napa Valley wineries.

Friday, April 27

8:00 a.m.	Limousine pick-up at hotel.
9:00 a.m.	Conference in executive suite.
	Each Executive VP will make a 30-minute presentation, followed by 15-minute Q & A.
1:00 p.m.	Catered lunch in executive suite.
2:00 p.m.	Meetings with company's technical advisors and department heads (Manufacturing, Finance, Customer Service, International Research and Development, Sales).

Saturday, April 28

8:00 a.m.	Farewell breakfast at hotel. Brief remarks by CEO.
10:45 a.m.	Limousine pick-up for airport.
1:00 p.m.	Universal flight #518, departs SFO for Paris.

Now John looks over the events that have been scheduled for the visit. He wants to be prepared for any foreseeable problems or opportunities.

3. LIST FORESEEABLE PROBLEMS AND OPPORTUNITIES

Since John is working from home this morning, he finds it easiest to use his computer rather than writing on a piece of paper. This way, John can quickly access his plan to make it happen while at lunch with the VP today. He'll pull it up on his smartphone using a mobile app. Later, John will be able to access it from his computer at work and can have his assistant print it out, or e-mail it, for distribution to colleagues and senior management who will be involved in the upcoming visit.

But not everyone wants to proceed online, use a smartphone app, or in any way continue this process on a computer-driven device. Many people still prefer to write out their plans. That's fine. It's nice to have options. The point is to stick to the process and not to skip a single step.

ENJOY THE JOURNEY

I've had many people tell me that this step—listing foreseeable problems and opportunities—is one of the most satisfying for them. Some even say it's fun! They told me that they liked playing devil's advocate.

Even better, these people told me that this step and the next step took away all their fears and worries. They felt great relief, knowing that they could face whatever happened with confidence, after completing this step and the next one.

My experience has been the same.

In this step, you review your action plan and then list all the foreseeable problems and opportunities that you can imagine might realistically occur. Don't go overboard here. Use common sense.

Here's what John comes up with.

FORESEEABLE PROBLEMS

• Visitor becomes ill

• Visitor gets lost

• Protestors at the airport

• Protestors at big dinner with mayor

• Visitors do not communicate in English well

• Freeway gridlock

FORESEEABLE OPPORTUNITIES

• Mayor's dinner goes well

• Build immediate French-American cultural bridges

• French-American celebrity is a hit with visitors

John feels really good at this point. In less than 30 minutes, half of his planning for the visit is done. But no time to sit back and relax. He is to have lunch with the VP in a few hours, so he presses on.

4. DEFINE ACTIONS TO PREVENT OR FACILITATE

Remember the athletic coach from an earlier chapter? He prepared his team ahead of time to meet foreseeable strategies by any opponent. That's what you must do here. You must define your response to all of the foreseeable problems and opportunities that you wrote down, one by one.

Some like to call this the "What-if" step.

With this critical step, you become like the coach who trains his team on what to do when the opponent uses different strategies to try and prevent his team from winning. He trains them in the "what-ifs" that his opponents might try.

This step enables you to be not merely aware of potential problems and opportunities, but to be able to address them in a heartbeat. Prepared for action. Bring it on. You'll be ready!

Let's see what John does here.

John writes his response to "what if" for each problem and opportunity he lists, as you can see:

FORESEEABLE PROBLEMS	PREVENTION OR FACILITATION
Visitor becomes ill	• Send weather forecast to visitors. • Select only highly rated restaurants.
Visitor gets lost	• Put local guide in each vehicle. • Make sure each driver has description and photo of visitors in that vehicle. • Require frequent head counts.

Protestors at airport	• Brief French official spokesperson ahead of time and prepare key talking points together. • Alert airport security of visit and possibility.
Protestors at big dinner with mayor	• Brief French official spokesperson ahead of time and prepare key talking points together. • Alert local police of visit and possibility.
Visitors do not communicate in English well	• Hire an interpreter for the initial airport arrival. • Alert interpreter to the possibility of a longer, multiday commitment.
Freeway gridlock	• Contact highway patrol. • Monitor news reports.
FORESEEABLE OPPORTUNITIES	
Mayor's dinner goes well	• Prep mayor on key interests of visitors. • Prepare mayor to present special city memento.
Build French-American cultural bridges	• Invite French-American celebrity to golf game. • Invite French-American singer to mayor's dinner.
French-American celebrity is a hit	• Get celebrity who is well recognized in France. • Prep celebrity on key interests of visitors.

John updates his action plan to reflect these preventive and facilitative actions.

Now John must create a Plan B so everyone will know what to do if things either don't go as planned, or if a hoped-for opportunity presents itself. He must also set alarm triggers so his team will know when it's time to execute Plan B.

But before we get to the last three steps of the plan to make it happen, I'd like you to take a look at one of your own concerns. Follow the questions below. It will make your planning very simple and easy!

DO IT:

Choose one of your Plan to Make It Happen concerns from your simplified Dump List, and answer the questions below. These questions reflect the steps you've just learned.

The Plan to Make It Happen concern I choose from my simplified Dump List is:

Good! Now, just follow the steps you learned previously—the same steps John followed.

What is your objective? Write your objective statement here:

Write out your action plan here:

- List all the foreseeable problems and opportunities you can think of on the left side of the space below.

"WHAT-IFS" PROBLEMS   SOLUTIONS
AND OPPORTUNITIES   TO EACH "WHAT-IF"

- Now go back and list the ways you will prevent or facilitate each "What-If" listed previously. Write your solution to the right of each item.

Be sure to update your action plan with your new preventive and facilitative actions.

Excellent job!

Look at your list. See how much progress you've made? You are almost finished with your planning. It was easy and simple. And you are feeling so much lighter that stress is becoming a thing of the past. But don't get too carried away here—you have three more steps to go.

You are ready to continue, as is John.

5. DEFINE BACK-UP (PLAN B) ACTIONS

We often joke about having a Plan B in our lives. But it's no joke. It's essential.

You already know from the athletic examples earlier that every good coach has a Plan B, and often a Plan C, D, and E as well. You don't need the extra plans, but you do need a Plan B. We'll call it a back-up plan ("B" for back-up).

"What's a back-up plan?" you ask. It's a good question. Most of us have a vague notion of what it is. We laugh about it in jokes. But I've taught many individuals who truly did not know what a back-up plan is, much less how to define one for a given situation.

Put simply, a back-up plan is what you do when some part of your original plan doesn't work out.

For example,

- What happens in a basketball game if your opponent doesn't opt to press your team man-to-man, but instead decides to use a zone defense?

- What happens if it rains on the day of your friend's outdoor wedding reception?

- What happens if it dumps 17 inches of snow and bizarre blizzard conditions on the first day of a national trade show convention? (This example did happen to a friend of mine, by the way, at a winter trade show in Maryland. The results were chaotic. The entire city shut down for two days.)

You get the picture.

So, let's look at John. What back-up plans does he define for each of the potential problems and opportunities that might come his way during the upcoming visit by the French officials?

WAIT A MINUTE!

Remember the quarterback (QB) in the heat of a football game? He shouts out audibles to his teammates to signal a change of plan. He lets them know, quickly, that they have to go for a Plan B in order to take advantage of a different strategy the opponent is using.

A good QB is adept at making good calls. He is able to size up in a nanosecond the opponents' play strategy and calls out which Plan B his team needs to execute.

Do you think the coach has prepared his team, and his QB, to know a Plan B for every play possible? You bet!

But if there's no QB to call out when it's time to use Plan B, then the team won't use Plan B. This is an essential point. You need a "trigger alarm" to shout out when it's time to go to Plan B.

A back-up plan is no good unless you know when to use it.

That's why Step 5 (Define Back-Up) and Step 6 (Create Trigger Alarms) are interconnected. You can't have one without the other.

Let's take a look.

6. CREATE TRIGGER ALERT

Trigger alerts are like the QB's audibles. They let you know when it's time to execute Plan B. When you plan ahead like this, you know ahead of time—just like the football team who listens to its QB—when it's time to put a back-up plan into place.

For example:

- Consider "what if" rain comes down in sheets on the day of your friend's outdoor wedding reception. A smart wedding or hotel planner would have already been prepared with either outdoor tents or an indoor room. He or she would have already addressed this back-up plan with you so that you would not be worried about it on the day of your special occasion. How does the planner know it's time to use the back-up plan? It rains! Rain is the trigger alert for the hotel to execute its back-up plan.

- Consider the 17-inch snow dump on the first day of a trade show mentioned earlier. In this case, no back-up plan had been made or discussed. The city did not even have enough snow plows to address the situation and had to scramble to contract with nearby cities to help out. It took two days to execute that frenetic nonplan. Nearly everything ground to a halt. The trade show hotel ran out of food. Guests braved the storm to walk to nearby restaurants that were open only incidentally because workers could not get home. People were stranded at airports.

  Obviously, in such an extreme (but true) example, some level of chaos would be expected no matter what. And luckily, no one starved, became ill, or was seriously injured to my knowledge. My friend tells me it turned out to be a fun, "bonding" experience for those already at the hotel, but a nightmare for others.

That said, a bit of reasonable back-up planning would have lessened the chaos. After all, the weather report did indicate a heavy snowstorm was predicted. No one expected 17 inches because that was not typical of even a heavy Baltimore storm at that time of year. Nonetheless, the hotel and city might have done a better job of at least having a Plan B if roads became thick with enough snow to leave people stranded and dependent on the hotel for food. When would the hotel know to execute Plan B? In this case, the relentless snow fall would have been the trigger alert!

- Consider someone living in California or Washington state, or Japan or Indonesia, areas prone to earthquakes. Would they be wise to do nothing at all to prepare for a major quake? No back-up plan. Not smart! In these cases, the trigger alert would be a major earthquake.

To sum up, Steps 5 (Back-Up Plan) and 6 (Trigger Alerts) are interconnected. A back-up plan, no matter how brilliant it is, won't be helpful if you don't have a trigger alert. And a trigger alert with no back-up plan is useless. You need both: Back-up plan and trigger alert!

Let me repeat that essential point:

YOU *ALWAYS* NEED BOTH A BACK-UP PLAN AND A TRIGGER ALERT!

DON'T STRESS OUT ABOUT PERFECTION HERE!

Sometimes people get hung up at this point. It always surprises me because so many people don't even plan at all. The people who I see getting hung up trying to devise the perfect back-up plan and trigger alert don't realize that they are already ahead of the game for even thinking about this. Yet I see them agonizing over options for a back-up plan and a trigger alert.

Trust me, there are no absolutes here.

Some plans are better than others. Some trigger alerts are more prudent than others. Some trigger alerts are more serious and impactful than others. But it's your call, and you need to have confidence in yourself and in your colleagues, to put together the best Plan B and trigger alerts you can come up with. Don't agonize over it.

After the fact, if you later realize that the Plan B you defined was not as good as another Plan B would have been, don't stress about it.

Life is a learning experience and you'll get better as you experience and learn about different unexpected situations.

Do you think a new QB is as sharp as a five-year veteran? Trust me, none of us is perfect the first time around, or even the tenth time around. Have you ever met a golfer or tennis player who didn't have room for improvement in his or her game? Of course not!

All of us, even those whom you admire most, get better as we learn from our less-than-perfect actions along the way. So do me a favor—don't stress out here.

Believe me, if you have prepared and written down a back-up plan and trigger alert ahead of time, you are already way ahead of most other people. Don't overdo it. Do the best you can with the tools you have. That's the important thing to remember.

Let's see what John defines as his back-up plan and trigger alert for each potential problem and opportunity he lists.

PROBLEMS	BACK-UP PLAN
Visitor becomes ill	• Drive to nearest hospital.
	• Have on-call doctor available.
	Alarm Trigger:
	• Visitor gets sick.
Visitor gets lost	• Immediately alert other vehicle drivers and John.
	• After 30-minute search, alert local police.
	• After 30-minute search, distribute lost visitor's description and last-seen location to media and police.
	Alarm Trigger (any one):
	• Someone not present for head count.
	• No one knows where that person is.
Protestors at airport	• Alert airport security to disband protestors.
	• Help airport security protect and guide group to safety.

Alarm Trigger:

- Demonstrators are loud and vocal, crowd growing before flight arrives.
- Reporters and camera crews seem hostile in their questions.

Protestors at big dinner with mayor

- Alert local police to disband protestors.
- Keep visitors inside until safe to exit.

Alarm Trigger:

- Demonstrators are loud and vocal, crowd growing before dinner.
- Reporters and camera crews seem hostile in their questions.

Visitors do not communicate in English well

- Have interpreter step in to help.

Alarm Trigger:

- Visitors can't communicate with hosts immediately upon arrival at airport.

Freeway gridlock

- Take alternative routes.

Alarm Trigger:

- News reports major gridlock; a call to highway patrol confirms it.
- GPS indicates a problem.

OPPORTUNITIES

Mayor's dinner goes well

- Have photographer to take photos.
- Send Twitter update, with photo (if possible).
- Write and send press release after dinner, with photo.

	Alarm Trigger (any one):
	• Mayor and visitors are clearly enjoying themselves.
	• Mayor and visitors have thanked you for event.
Build French-American cultural bridges	• Have photographer take pictures.
	• Twitter.
	• Submit press release after dinner.
	• Submit article to French-American community newsline.
	Alarm Trigger:
	• Visitors clearly enjoy French-American celebrity.
	• Visitors and French-American celebrity share similar passion for their homeland.
French-American celebrity is a hit	• Have photographer take pictures.
	• Twitter.
	Alarm Trigger:
	• Visitors clearly enjoy French-American celebrity.
	• Visitors and French-American celebrity share similar passion for their homeland.

John doesn't want anything to get forgotten. He quickly adds his back-up plans and alarm triggers to his action plan. This way, these actions will be ready to go and at his fingertips, just in case.

Done! In less than an hour, John is ready to present his plans to the VP.

See how easy that was?

7. UPDATE YOUR ACTION PLAN

You may have noticed that John updated his action plan after every step. But you'd be shocked to learn how many people do a great job in their plan to make it happen, and then forget to update their action plan. I'm always amazed by this.

Obviously, all the preparation and alternative plans in the world are worthless if nothing is added to your action plan. What if you run into trouble, or extraordinary success, along the way? No one will know how to handle these things if they aren't in the action plan.

In John's case, how will his team know when it's time to call the photographer or doctor, or to call the police if necessary? Will they have these phone numbers at their fingertips, or will they have to scramble for them in a moment of chaos?

As your coach, I want to make sure you update *your* action plan!

Luckily, John knows this well. He now takes all the preventive and facilitative actions, and all of his back-up plans and trigger alerts, and adds them to his action plan. His plan is updated and current.

Here's an example of what just one of his action plan entries now looks like:

Wednesday, April 25

6 p.m.	• Reception and Dinner with San Francisco mayor at Top of the Mark.
	• Prep mayor on key interests of visitors.
	• Prepare mayor to present special city memento.

BACK-UP PLAN

- Have photographer take pictures.
- Twitter.
- Submit press release after dinner.

- Write and send press release after dinner with photo.

Alarm Trigger:

- Mayor and visitors are clearly enjoying themselves.

All the anxiety John felt at first about being asked to manage and plan the French officials' visit is gone. He knows the VP will be pleased with his plan. And, even better, John now feels confident that he is well prepared for the visit. He knows that he is well prepared to handle any foreseeable mishap and to take advantage of any opportunity to garner good publicity as well.

DO IT:

Now you are ready to finish your Plan to Make It Happen.

Remember, you're going to define your Back-Up Plan and Trigger Alert for each potential problem and opportunity.

I have confidence in you! Go for it.

On the left side of the following blank spaces, list your Foreseeable Problems and Opportunities.

When you are through, go back and write your Back-up Plan if things go awry, (or well), and your Trigger Alert to let you know when you need to shift to Plan B.

FORESEEABLE PROBLEMS AND OPPORTUNITIES	BACK-UP PLAN AND TRIGGER ALERT

Wow! You're done! You did it! Now put these items into your Action Plan.

You completed your Plan to Make It Happen! Excellent job! You now can execute any dream or project with confidence, a confidence that will inspire others to follow you, to want to be part of your team.

REMEMBER:

- In order to Plan to Make It Happen, just follow the following seven easy steps:

  1. State the objective

  2. Develop an action plan

  3. List foreseeable problems and opportunities

  4. Define how to prevent or facilitate

  5. Define back-up ("Plan B")

  6. Create trigger alerts

  7. Update your action plan

  PLAN TO MAKE IT HAPPEN

Chapter Ten

GO FORWARD WITH CONFIDENCE

Playing safe is probably the most unsafe thing in the world. You cannot stand still. You must go forward.

—Robert Collier

We should regret our mistakes and learn from them, but never carry them forward into the future with us.

—Lucy Maud Montgomery

Enduring setbacks while maintaining the ability to show others the way to go forward is a true test of leadership.

—Nitin Nohria

Having thus chosen our course, without guile and with pure purpose, let us renew our trust in God, and go forward without fear.

—Abraham Lincoln

Confidence is contagious and so is the lack of confidence.

—Vince Lombardi

One cursory reading of this little, practical book will not make you a "master" in anything. Of course not.

But even one reading of this system will put you far ahead of where you were just a few hours ago. It will put you far ahead of others around you who struggle with information overload, additional responsibilities thanks to "right-sizing," multiple projects for home, work, and personal life. Yes, you are already on your way to a calmer and more productive future.

Remember where you were before you read these pages, before you learned this simple, easy system for handling even the most difficult and seemingly impossible "mountains"?

I assure you. Right now, you are in a much different place than you were before.

And that's a good thing, a very good thing.

Now, as your patient and respectful coach—as a seasoned mentor who has helped tens of thousands of executives and nonexecutives around the world achieve their dreams simply by using the system you just learned—I heartily encourage you to use this book as your sure guide for truly mastering decision making, problem solving, and planning.

Go forward with confidence!

DO IT:

Go to a calendar right now and first mark off 30 days and then 60 days from today. Put a note on these two dates that reads: "Send Guy a note."

Now you must refer to this book as often as needed and use this system every day, whether your mountains are big or little. This will give you practice and experience. The system will begin to feel like second nature to you.

Then, at the end of 30 days, drop me a note to let me know the biggest change you've noticed so far.

Don't quit. If one day you forget, no problem; just pick yourself up and use the system in the book the next day or the next hour. Weave it into the very fabric of your thinking, into the fabric of your approach to anything that comes up.

Continue to use this system daily, referring as often as needed to this book.

Then, in 60 days, write me another quick note to let me know the biggest improvements you've noticed in your life since you started using this system.

REMEMBER:

Now, my dear friend, you will be well on your way to mastering *Think Fast!*

Before this year's end, I would not be surprised to learn that your colleagues and family are commenting about how different you seem, how confident and stress-free you have become, how much you are accomplishing these days, yet in such a calm manner that you make it look easy.

Others are beginning to ask *you* for advice and direction in handling their own concerns. They are commenting to their peers that they want to learn your secret to success and achievement.

It's a good feeling, isn't it?

It's nice to be on this side of the mountain!

But at this point in your journey, it's difficult to imagine not using this system. It's difficult to even recall how chaotic your life felt only a year ago. What a relief!

GO FORWARD WITH CONFIDENCE

INNOVATION:
CREATE SOMETHING NEW

Innovation is the ability to see change as an opportunity—not a threat.

—Thomas Edison

Innovation is not the product of logical thought, although the result is tied to logical structure.

—Albert Einstein

Learning and innovation go hand in hand. The arrogance of success is to think that what you did yesterday will be sufficient for tomorrow.

—William Pollard

A dream with courage is innovation . . .
A dream without courage is a delusion.

—Anonymous

I believe in being an innovator.

—Walt Disney

S ometimes a concern just doesn't fit into the box, so to speak. It needs to be resolved, yet it doesn't quite require the "Decide Now" skills. Nor does it exactly require the skills to "Find Out Why" or to "Make It Happen." At the same time, elements of each of the three thinking skills are required to resolve this outside-the-box concern.

If you have such a concern on your simplified Dump List, it's a pretty sure indication you need to create something new; you need to innovate.

Pioneering medical doctors and researchers, Research & Development (R&D) departments, entrepreneurs, teachers, busy moms, Olympic skiers, and top golfers—actually, all of us at one time or another—must innovate.

This is always a fun chapter for us to teach. Here's why.

Whenever I begin to talk about this skill, two distinct reactions quickly show up on the faces of my audience. It doesn't matter if I'm training senior management, CEOs and

VPs, athletic coaches, or blue-collar workers. I always notice the same, distinct two reactions: delight in the eyes and on the faces of some in the room, and "Oh, no, this isn't for me," in the eyes and on the faces of the rest. This split reaction is so predictable that my colleagues and I now anticipate it with good humor.

The good news is that no matter which side of the room you identify with, the end result is the same for all: satisfaction that they, too, have finally learned a simple way to ignite and resolve successful innovation.

So, how does it work?

Before I show you, I want to emphasize that all of us—*every single one of us*—must innovate, create something new, fairly often in our lives.

Creating something new doesn't have to mean inventing something new from the ground up, starting at zero. Usually it's relatively simple, common sense, such as inventing a new way to do something routine; discovering a new, effective use for a tool; finding a shortcut to work in the morning that avoids most of the traffic. All innovations.

Consider these examples:

A good coach has to focus on more than practiced plays for a game. He has to know more than technique and skills, and his opponents' plays. He also has to incite his team members to give their all, every play, every game. He has to motivate them to *want* to play together as a team, to *want* to win, to respect each other, and even to enjoy the journey together.

This is no small project . Working with emotions and feelings and radically different personalities is not at all like working with numbers. You have to be present to the moment, you have to be sensitive to the vibe, and you have to be innovative in guiding a team to move, think, act, and win as a cohesive whole.

The winningest active NBA coach of the Los Angeles Lakers, Phil Jackson, talks about his secrets to building a team in his interviews. Think about it, a major league coach in any sport has to bring his team together, yet still inspire individuals, while guiding a group of high-energy, highly talented, highly paid young men or women—each radically different in personality from one another—to be both leaders and team players rather than to play as isolated individuals. That's quite a challenge, wouldn't you say?

As Phil Jackson himself put it, in his book, *Sacred Hoops*:

> Basketball is a sport that involves the subtle interweaving of players at full speed to the point where they are thinking and moving as one.

What he did with two teams, the Lakers and the Chicago Bulls, is to turn them around completely. These two teams, under Jackson's direction, transformed from being a team with super-watt stars and mega-talent but no cohesiveness, no sense of "team" and few wins, to being a team in which all players— big stars and rookies—focus on the *team* outcome and, in a relatively short time, become winners of championships.

Like many other extraordinary coaches, innovation was Jackson's strong suit. He had to think outside the traditional coaching box to achieve this feat. So have many others before and after him, in every sport imaginable.

Jackson calls his approach spiritual, getting individual players to think outside themselves, to focus as a team on something greater than themselves, and to become team-oriented, unselfish.

Without getting sidetracked on the specifics of his approach, news stories about this winning coach taking his team on a fun outing at a local boardwalk the day before a big game are common. When you read a story like that, the first thing that strikes you is, "Wow, who would have thought of that?" But then something in your mind relates to it. It makes sense; doing something fun and goofy, as a team, couldn't help but relax everyone and put team players in a good mood—a good, relaxed, had-fun-together, team mentality that they'll need to draw on the next night when every muscle and every thought will be focused on winning an important game.

Then again, consider a friend of mine who is in the life sciences industry. He's helped bring more than 20 medical devices to market, and a number of them are life-saving. That's a remarkable record.

It's fascinating to listen to him explain the newest device and its use. I find myself always amazed at how this new invention came about. Sometimes a researcher was seeking a solution to a specific difficulty, and a pattern emerged which led the inventor to discover the new invention. Other times a scientist is looking for one thing and discovers something astounding and different along the way.

But I'm also fascinated with my friend's innovative skills. He is not the inventor of these devices. Instead he leads these companies. Without his business and industry savvy, these brilliant new inventions would never see the light of day. This friend finds ways to fund the multimillions of dollars of research and development, to coordinate the required (and often complicated) testing and approval processes, and to strategize marketing. Innovation is a critical component of the inventor's new product, as well as of my friend's corporate leadership.

So, you might be wondering, what's the secret process to always deliver good innovation? There isn't one. At least there isn't a process.

My colleagues and I spent years observing and experimenting with different processes we came up with. But none delivered fool-proof innovation *every* time.

That was puzzling. Illusive.

Clearly all of us innovate, sometimes daily, and often without even giving it a second thought. Why isn't there a method or system to ensure good innovation *every* time?

After a long while, I came back at the issue in a different way.

OBSERVATION YIELDS RESULTS

Although there was not a process that could guarantee good innovative results every time, there did seem to be a pattern.

Every opportunity I could find, I tested and refined the pattern I saw. Yes. It seemed to be consistent. Then, in working with more than 100 companies—large and small—during the past several years, I identified and confirmed that there are six key principles to successful innovation.

In every successful innovation I examined, these six principles were integral to its success. In every new innovation I led or guided, these same six principles were integral to the new innovation's breakthrough nature and to its success.

These six principles (principles, not "steps") are:

1. Extend It Forward
2. Champion
3. Avoid the Corporate Swamp
4. Attract Allies
5. Find a Sponsor
6. Fulfill Necessity

Don't think of these principles as steps, for they are sometimes executed simultaneously or in a different order. That's why I did not number these principles 1 to 6. You see, innovation does not follow a process, such as those you've learned for good, consistent decision making, problem solving, and planning. These innovation principles are not steps in a process.

Instead, think of these principles as the solid and necessary foundation for innovation.

Imagine a house. You can't build a strong, secure house if you don't start with a strong, secure, and adequate foundation. The entire structure of the house is only as good as the foundation upon which it rests. Yes, building materials are important too, but if the foundation is bad, then the best housing materials in the world won't keep the house from eventually crumbling.

A builder can make the walls of a house before he lays the foundation. Pre-fabricated (pre-fab) houses can be built this way. And if you've ever volunteered for a house-building charity such as Corazon, you know that while some volunteers are clearing the land and laying the foundation, others are painting the very simple house siding and building the wall frames. But none of these house components—wall frames, siding, windows, or doors—will be stable and firm without a solid foundation.

These six principles of innovation are like the solid, strong foundation of a house. Rely on them in every innovation you pursue and you are sure to experience success.

Let's examine these principles more closely.

1. EXTEND IT FORWARD

I've been privy to witnessing the development of many innovations, in many different kinds of industries, over the years. To my surprise, I observed that in all these innovations and in all the innovations I researched, nothing comes from nothing. This is true even for the biggest innovations you can think of. All innovations begin where something else ended. I call this principle "extend it forward" because every innovation is an extension of something that already exists.

Think about it. Think of the innovations you see around you. An innovation might take someone else's idea to new heights, or apply it to a new purpose. Look at major innovations throughout history, such as developments in fighter jets or cruise ships, the wheel, the automobile, industrial automation, radio, television, hair and grooming products, software, video games, smartphones, social networking, and more. All of these innovations improved upon something that came before.

Some innovations created whole new industries around them, such as the automobile, industrial automation, radio, television, and the Internet. Even so, none of these innovations began in isolation. Each one built upon something that came before it.

But . . .

Yes, I can hear you asking yourself, "What about copyright infringement and intellectual property rights?" Please don't confuse "infringing on someone else's intellectual property" with "innovation."

In the race to be first and to have a competitive edge in publicly introducing a new innovation, I've seen competitors introduce a new product to market before the originator is able to launch his original invention. That's tough. But it's the way of life these days.

Patents, trademarks, and copyrights offer some protection. But even with protection, it takes the competition a little over 18 months to reverse engineer a new product and avoid copyright issues. A new service has even less of a chance to keep competition at bay. On average, a new service is copied within six months if it is an innovation.

Do you see why I say "nothing comes from nothing"?

Let's say you feel that you are on to something new, something that might be commercially successful. What can you do to protect your innovation while it is incubating and before you are ready to launch?

One thing you can do to keep your innovation hidden from competitive eyes and yet still test it out, is to have trusted friends test and refine it for you before you launch it. You can even reward them in some way, maybe with a gift card (a good innovation), to say "thank you!"

Your insider group of trusted friends may think of a new approach to make your innovation more useful. They will tell you what they like and what they don't like, and give you suggestions for improvement. Major companies do this all the time.

For example, before the first iPhone hit the stores, before a word about this innovation was even breathed to the media, trusted Apple employees tested it out. For months upon months these trusted employees used the product, gave suggestions for improvements, gave feedback about what they did and did not like, and generally served as the first beta test market for this innovation.

You may remember a few years later, prior to the release of the fourth generation iPhone, a scandal broke out when one of the beta testers accidentally left his beta iPhone 4 at a local pub. The phone made its way into the hands of a reporter. Of course, the resulting news article quickly hit mainstream media on the Internet, TV, radio, and in print. Overnight international news. It was an accidental slip. But Apple sure wasn't happy about it.

Once a product or service is launched and has proven to be a commercial success, the only way to keep a competitive advantage is to continue to innovate. See for yourself by observing the multitude of big-name corporate innovations you see advertised or in the news every month. Every month we learn about new and better pharmaceuticals, new clothing styles, new cooking recipes, and new diets. Industry trade journals keep tabs of innovations within their fields. The industry leaders keep innovating. They have to. Nothing comes from nothing. Extend it forward.

Okay. You have an innovation. How many innovations never see the light of day? There's a reason for that. No one championed them!

2. CHAMPION

Every innovation needs a champion in order to succeed. You must champion your innovation. But the skills required to bring something to market are different from those that were used to develop the innovation in the first place. Both skill sets are important. And the innovator is frequently the best champion of his or her innovation. But not always.

There are literally millions of great new ideas generated every day throughout the world, but very few of them attain commercial success.

Consider Steve Jobs and Steve Wozniak, co-founders of Apple, Inc. Both were innovators. And both were remarkable champions of their early Macintosh products. Even so, a fellow named Guy Kawasaki is the one who really put Apple on the map in the early days. He was a champion for the new product, even though he did not invent it. Kawasaki has written books on the topic and has gone on to champion other innovations since then. His success and approach to championing a product are studied in many college marketing classes, as you may already know.

Put simply: No champion. No success. No matter how terrific an innovation might be!

3. AVOID THE CORPORATE SWAMP

As strange as this sounds, every company, every organization, every municipality, every group of people has what I call a "corporate swamp." This is where good ideas die.

In a sense, companies are like human bodies. They reject anything that is different from the original organism. Companies typically reject new ideas and anything that will cause them to perform differently.

Let me give you some examples.

I used to travel to Australia frequently. During one visit with a few leading companies down under, a phrase that these executives used caught my ears. They spoke of the "tall poppy syndrome."

The tall poppy syndrome refers to the common reality that in a field of poppies, the tallest one stands out and gets its head picked off first. Applying that concept to the realm of business or everyday life, people tend to try and destroy the "tall poppy" within any group. A person who brings innovation to an organization is obviously a "tall poppy." He or she stands out from the norm of the group or organization culture.

You can see the same tall poppy syndrome in a group of immature teens—boys or girls. The one who is different gets kicked out of the "in" crowd, so to speak.

Is it jealousy, laziness, or fear that causes the corporate swamp mentality? I don't know. As far as I'm concerned, it's just life. It's just how it is. There is a natural resistance to innovation, so be aware and don't get sucked into the corporate swamp mentality.

Here is one more example. I hope you enjoy its light-hearted approach as much as I do. I find that the corporate swamp mentality—and its innovation-stunting results—is captured amusingly and well in the lyrics from the popular Broadway musical entitled, *How to Succeed in Business Without Really Trying* (music and lyrics by Frank Loesser, book by Abe Burrows).

In this musical, an enterprising young man, who is eager to advance his career, starts out by working in the mailroom of a large company. He asks advice of the man who is the director of the mailroom.

In response, the mailroom director—a man who has worked in the exact same position for 25 years—boasts of his job security and stability. He tells the young man that the secret of his success is that he does everything according to "the company policy, the company way." (I'd call this the corporate swamp mentality!) Of course, it's the exact opposite of what the innovative young man wants to do.

Some of the mailroom director's corporate swamp advice are expressed in these lyrics:

As a brash young man, "Well," I said to myself,
"Now, brash young man,

Don't get any ideas." Well, I stuck to that,
and I haven't had one in years.

. . . I play it the company way;
Wherever the company puts me, there I stay.

. . . I have no point of view.

The young man is shocked. He asks a series of incredulous questions, to which the mailroom director responds in a way that absolutely confirms his corporate swamp philosophy. The lyrics continue:

Young man: Supposing the company thinks . . .

Mailroom director: I think so too.

Young man: Now, what would you say . . . ?

Mailroom director: I wouldn't say.

Young man: Your face is a company face.

Mailroom director: It smiles at executives,

then goes back in place.

Young man: The company furniture?

Mailroom director: Oh, it suits me fine.

Young man: The company letterhead?

Mailroom director: A valentine.

Young man: Anything you're against?

Mailroom director: Unemployment.

Young man: When they want brilliant thinking
from employees?

Mailroom director: That is no concern of mine.

Young man: Suppose a man of genius makes suggestions?

Mailroom director: Watch that genius get suggested to resign.

Young man: So you play it the company way?

Mailroom director: All company policy is by me okay.

Young man: You'll never rise up to the top!

Mailroom director: But there's one thing clear:

Whoever the company fires,

I will still be here.

Young man: Oh, you certainly found a home!

Mailroom director: It's cozy.

Young man: Your brain is a company brain.

Mailroom director: The company washed it,
now I can't complain.

. . . Young man: The company restaurant?

Mailroom director: Ev'ry day same lunch:

Their haddock sandwich; it's delicious!

Young man: Do you have any hobbies?

Mailroom director: I've a hobby; I play gin with Mr. Bratt.

Young man: Mr. Bratt! And do you play it nicely?

Mailroom director: Play it nicely . . . still,
he blitzes me in every game, like that!

Young man: Why?

Mailroom director: 'Cause I play it the company way.
Executive policy is by me okay.

Young man: Oh, how can you get anywhere?

Mailroom director: Junior, have no fear;
Whoever the company fires, I will still be here.

Young man: You will still be here . . . .
Year after year after fiscal, never take a risk—all year!

. . . Mailroom director: I will someday earn my medal:
Twenty-five year employee.

I'll see to it that the medal is the only thing they'll ever
pin on me.

The Frump way is the company way. Executive policy
is by him okay.

I'll never be president, but there's one thing clear,
as long as my uncle can stand me,

I will still be here.

Of course this is a little extreme, but you clearly get the idea
of what I mean by getting stuck in the corporate swamp .

Don't do it!

4. ATTRACT ALLIES

In strategizing how to get a new idea, an innovation, into an organization, it's critical to have allies, true believers who will also promote it to decision makers.

The time to line up allies is *before* launching a product or service, and before promoting your corporate innovation to higher-ups. You must figure out who is likely to embrace your innovation, and avoid those who are stuck in the company swamp.

Allies are people within an organization who are its true leaders when it comes to strategic thinking.

Allies are like offensive linemen in football. Your innovation is like the football, and you are like the quarterback. You need the offensive linemen to block the naysayers and swamp dwellers so that you can at least make a pass to the end zone.

Once you've lined up key allies for your innovation, influencers who agree at least to help keep others from blocking a consideration of your innovation as it is presented to the decision makers, then you're ready for your champion to carry the ball.

Remember, as uncomfortable as it might make you to attract allies, you must do it for your innovation to have a chance at success.

5. FIND A SPONSOR

No surprise here. Without some degree of financing or resources, however minimal they might be, it's nearly impossible to succeed with any innovation.

Sponsors are those in an organization who can support your champion with a budget, with free time to experiment or create a prototype, and with the tools or financing to go forward. Typically such an organizational sponsor will be in senior management and responsible for overseeing and expanding the company's competitive edge.

Too often, innovators within an organization can't find a sponsor to help get an innovation out of the corporate swamp. That's why you frequently see an innovator leaving a company and starting his or her own start-up company.

Even a breakaway entrepreneur needs funding. Angel investors, venture capitalists, foundation grants, friends, and family are all among the resources an entrepreneur will use to find sponsors.

Yes, the entrepreneur's original employer may have lost out on a terrific new innovation that could have generated new and abundant streams of income for the company. But, c'est la vie. The innovator who is a true believer in the value of his innovation must move on. He must find one or several sponsors in order to bring his innovation to the public.

Consider the explosive growth of Facebook, for example. Who ever heard of "social networking," let alone Facebook, just a few years before it was publicly introduced? Yet it is one of the fastest growing innovations ever.

Within its first seven years (2004–2011), Facebook grew to 600 million active users. That is a remarkable achievement.

When you look at Facebook's development behind the scenes, before it ever hit the marketplace, you'll see that Facebook had all of the principles I've given you in this chapter. The six principles of innovation were Facebook's foundation and a big part of the reason for its phenomenal success.

Let me explain.

In the Facebook example, behind the scenes, several inventors were involved. According to the movie *The Social Network*, these young Harvard student inventors included the Winklevoss twins, Tyler and Cameron, and Mark Zuckerberg.

The invention is great. But the inventors need an ally to get their invention off the ground. They find an ally in a man named Eduardo Saverin, Mark Zuckerberg's roommate. He gives the Facebook inventors just enough seed money to form a company and to seek out advertisers and promoters.

Ah, but they lack a champion.

Once the fledgling company hooks up with Sean Parker, then they have their champion and a chance to achieve huge commercial success. Without this champion, it is doubtful that Facebook would have achieved its phenomenal success. But at this point in its development, even with a champion, Facebook does not yet have enough for success. It needs a sponsor.

Venture capitalists step into the sponsor role. They like the innovation and think it is worth an investment risk. College students quickly prove that the investment was well placed. There is clearly a need for such an innovation.

Read on to learn about the sixth principle of Innovation.

6. FULFILL NECESSITY

At the beginning of this section, I told you that everyone can be, and is, innovative. All you need to do is look around you, at your friends, family members, and colleagues, and even at your own innovative moments, to know it's true.

Yes, innovation is around us daily. But it is in moments of hardship that this is especially true. Some refer to this phenomenon with the saying:

Necessity is the mother of invention.

In times of financial recession, for example, you'll find millions of people out of work. Yet these people still have to provide for their families, keep a roof over their heads, and survive. Many in this situation will do almost anything for pay while they look for work.

These people hit hardest by a recession often find themselves doing things they never would have imagined they'd be doing just a few years ago. Of course, I'm not talking about immoral or unethical activities. I'm referring to the engineer who finds himself checking groceries for awhile until he can find another engineering opportunity, or the VP of Marketing who takes on an assignment with a friend's start-up tech company for nominal compensation or part ownership of the company.

If you've experienced a sudden layoff, or have walked with a friend or relative or colleague who has been in this position, you know what I mean. It just "is what it is." Companies have to do what they can to survive, just the same as we do.

But amid the pain, there can be something exciting, fresh, and new. The hidden silver linings amid such struggles are the innovations that arise from necessity. Sometime recessions and down times foster whole new industries. It's like new flowers and tree branches that bloom most abundantly and brilliantly after a cold, harsh winter.

In a free marketplace, whenever there is a severe downturn in the economy, many people become entrepreneurs and innovators in order to find new ways to provide for their families. Many new companies and industries are created as a result of downsizing or "right-sizing."

If you're a corporate decision maker, especially if you are in charge of business development and growth, then you're always on the lookout for new companies and innovations to keep you ahead of the competition. You know that you can use the abundant new growth of such innovations during a down economy as a positive advantage. It's a great win-win opportunity. Perhaps your company will purchase or partner with a former employee's new start-up innovation. Perhaps you will hire an innovator to create a new division within your organization. These opportunities and innovations may never have seen the light of day if they'd gone through normal company ranks. But now your decision-making colleagues can clearly see the value of this or that new innovation to its bottom line.

Of course, a company doesn't have to lay people off to experience the benefits of innovation. Instead, a company can create an innovation fast-track that will foster and reward any employee who submits their innovation. A company can structure this innovation fast-track in such a way that it completely avoids the corporate swamp and immediately reaches open-minded decision makers.

Can you imagine what a boon of encouragement it is for employees to be told that their innovative ideas are so valued by a company that they will be rewarded and credited for any innovation they submit? No holds barred! Wow! Refreshing, isn't it?

In sum, follow these six principles of innovation and you will be on the pioneering fast-track yourself.

Enjoy the journey!

Index

ALAMO
LEARNING SYSTEMS

Alamo Learning Systems has trained tens of thousands of people, both in the United States and internationally, in the skills you have read about in *Think Fast!* We have several key supporting aids and reinforcement learning activities for those who wish to become proficient in these skills. Specifically, we offer the following to companies:

- In-house workshops
- Train-the-trainer workshops for companies that wish to become licensed to train their own people. The graduates receive a Process Master Certificate once they pass this course.

For individuals we offer:

- Downloadable worksheets of each of the four processes taught in *Think Fast!*
- Electronic coaching worksheets. These aids will ask you the process questions so that you can fill in the data for each process step.
- Certified e-learning course. This state-of-the-art training program will give you a good, in-depth understanding of all the skills taught in *Think Fast!* The content is adaptable to any level of expertise and learning style.

Please go to our website, www.alamols.com, for more information about how you can purchase these valuable supporting tools. You can also follow us on Twitter at AlamoLS and Facebook at Alamo Learning Systems.

Printed and bound by CPI Group (UK) Ltd, Croydon, CR0 4YY

13/04/2025

14656499-0001